PERSONAL POWER

*An Unorthodox
Guide to Success*

PERSONAL POWER

An Unorthodox Guide to Success

H. B. Karp, Ph.D.

GARDNER PRESS, INC.
Lake Worth, Florida

This book is dedicated to **Moe** and **Kate,** who got me started, and to **Jeri** and **Eric,** who keep me going.

Library of Congress Cataloging in Publication Data

Karp, H. B.
  Personal power.

  Includes index.
  1. Interpersonal relations. 2. Success.
3. Control (Psychology) I. Title.
HM132.K36 1985   302   84-45789
ISBN 0-89876-226-X

GARDNER PRESS, INC.
6801 Lake Worth Road
Lake Worth, FL 33467

The quotation at the beginning of Chapter 10 is taken from "The Merry Little Minuet" (Sheldon Harnick) © Copyright 1958—Alley Music Corp. and Trio Music Co., Inc. All rights administered by Hudson Bay Music, Inc.

Printing number

10 9 8 7 6 5 4 3 2 1

Preface

*Success is a journey
not a destination.*

Before you start reading this book, there are a few things that I would like to say to you, by way of introduction. I hope to orient you to my way of thinking a little before exposing you to it.

Power, to most people, is a very awesome word and subject. For some it conjures up images of torchlight parades, godlike individuals, and huge nations or organizations locked in mortal combat to determine which will be dominant. For others the word *power* suggests evil brilliance, deviousness, and political machinations. To be one of the powerful is to be a member of a very small but extremely elite circle of individuals who control the destinies of the uninformed masses.

Power is also considered by many to be very complex; they feel that in order to understand power, it is necessary to first have a basic understanding of psychology and a knowledge of history. In other words, it's possible to understand power, but only in terms of complex models and in psychosocial jargon and frames of reference.

Then there's my view.

I believe that power is simply part and parcel of everyone's day-to-day existence. Power, as I see it, is no more or less complicated than love, fun, effectiveness, or anything else that contributes to an individual's capacity for good living. The only thing that makes power stand out among all other human capacities is that it has become so misunderstood.

Although I am addressing this book to today's managers, I am doing so with the view that people are managers only eight hours a day. At the end of the work day, managers leave their offices and resume their roles as parents, spouses, or friends. Since power is just as important in these settings as it is in the work setting, my anecdotes come from all these environments.

Another aspect of this book that I would like to talk about here is its style. I did not sit down at my desk one day to write a book on power. Even now, the thought of doing something like that is a little frightening to me. What I did was sit down and *talk* with you about power, as if we were in a workshop together or were swapping war stories in an informal setting. In other words, I wrote this as if we were speaking together, face to face. I avoided jargon and complex models as much as possible. Where I used a specialized term, I defined it. I used some hypothetical illustrations, but for the most part I drew examples and illustrations from my own work and home life, including a couple of incidents where I really screwed things up.

I also want to mention that the ideas in this book are based on Gestalt theory. I think that it is important for me to inform you of this at the outset so that you can see my theory base clearly as you read. The book focuses strictly on the subject of power. The brief chapter on theory deals with *applied* theory and relates specifically to the aspects of power.

This book makes a statement about how I see power and its settings. Certainly I have been influenced by others along the way, and this influence may or may not be apparent. The few quotes that I used in the text of the book, with the exception of the definitions of power in Chapter 1, are ones that I remembered as I was writing this. I specifically avoided reading and discussing others' views on power as I worked on this, first, because others can express their own views much better than I can, and second, because this is my statement on power and I can express my own views much better than anyone can.

Contents

CHAPTER 1

An Introduction to Power

Of all the topics that have fascinated people about themselves over the centuries, the study of power and its uses has probably been the number one area of interest. From Machiavelli's *The Prince* down through current best sellers about power, people seem to be universally drawn to the subject. I know that this is true for me, or I wouldn't be writing this book, and I suspect that it's true for you, or you wouldn't be reading it.

Their Definitions

Regardless of the society that is referred to or the historical period in which power is discussed, the one common factor among all the old and present-day theorists and practitioners of power is that they invariably see power as an *interpersonal* dynamic. That is, at least two people are required for any expression of power. Most definitions of power speak in terms of political functions, autocratic leadership, or imposing one's will on other people.

Several current definitions underscore the point. In their study of power and society, Laswell and Kaplan define the relationship between power and political science: "Political science . . . is the study of the shaping and sharing of power." Renowned sociologist Max Weber states, "Power is the probability that one actor within a social relationship will be in a position to carry out his own will despite resistance, regardless of the basis on which this probability exists." The *International Encyclopedia of the Social Sciences* says, "Power refers to subsets of relations among social units such that behaviors of one or more units depend, in some circumstances, on the behavior of the other units." Webster's Third International Dictionary defines power as "the ability to compel obedience." Many psychologists see power simply as a basic human drive. All in all, these are old and frightening definitions that conjure up images of domination or "power over" someone else. I would like to introduce you to a radical departure from the conventional views and definitions.

My Definition

I contend that power is strictly an *intrapersonal* phenomenon requiring no one but you to exercise it fully. The expression of power is not subject to the external influence of others; furthermore, power is actually lost when it is seen as an interpersonal dynamic or a group activity.

Before I go on, a clear definition of the word *power* is needed. I define *power* simply as the ability to get all of what you want from the environment, given what's available. This definition comprises several parts, each of which requires a brief explanation.

First, power is cast in terms of a single human dimension—the individual's ability. This places complete responsibility for getting what you want squarely on you. If you gain an objective, you are powerful. If you are unsuccessful in an attempt to gain an objective, instead of asking, "Why won't those selfish people give me what I want?" the key question becomes, "How did I stop myself from getting what I wanted?" This view of taking complete responsibility for getting all of what you want pertains even to situations where someone else's compliance or help may be necessary. If you need the support or permission of someone else to accomplish something and you fail to get it, instead of castigating the other person for being stubborn or autocratic, you gain much more control in the situation by getting in touch with what *you* might have done differently.

Second, the object of power is not another individual. The object of power is to get something that you want, frequently from another person, that is of specific value to you. Therefore, power is not an end in itself but a process that has meaning or relevance only in terms of gaining results or achieving objectives. Power can be measured objectively in the number of personal or organizational goals attained. The pursuit of power for its own sake has little to recommend it as a healthy or productive pastime. As a matter of fact, pursuing power for its own sake, without a clear objective in mind, makes as much sense as pursuing gasoline for its own sake and not owning a car.

The third element in the definition involves the last phrase, "given what's available." Each individual has responsibility for, and control over, exactly one human being in this universe—himself or herself! To exercise power effectively, you must, as a first step, realize how much of what you want is actually available and attainable from the environment. Suppose you want a local dignitary to address your group on a specific date and he informs you that he is simply not available. Any further pursuit of this particular objective is not an exercise of power but a venture in futility. In not getting what you want in this case, you have not overestimated your power; you have simply learned that what you wanted was unavailable.

Just as it is important to define power in terms of what it is, it is important to define power in terms of what it is not. Power is not domination. Although these two terms are often confused and used interchangeably, there is no similarity between them and a clear distinction can be made between them.

First, the objective of power is to gain an end result; the objective of domination is to bend someone else to your will. Second, power is an intrapersonal phenomenon that requires only one individual, the person who wants something. Domination is an interpersonal phenomenon that requires at least two people, the "bender" and at least one "bendee."

Third, power tends to strengthen you and others, whereas domination weakens you and others. When you are powerful, you are getting what you want by relying on your own resources and judgment. This, of course, includes situations where you elicit the support and help of others. In being powerful, you strengthen yourself and at the same time give this message to others: "I'm pursuing my objectives, and if you want to attain your objectives, *you* are going to have to pursue them." Your power is always measured against *your* own performance.

Domination, on the other hand, is specifically geared to keeping other people weak, ineffective, or dependent, and all acts of domination are in the service of attaining one or all of these ends. Whereas your power is measured against your past performance, that is, yourself against yourself, domination can be measured only by how others are doing in relation to what you are doing, that is, yourself against others. To be powerful, you focus on beating your own past performance. To be dominant, you only have to be better than the next best. That is, if you have beaten everyone into submission, you don't have to be strong, you just have to be a little less weak than the next-weakest person. This is why bullies tend to crumble at the first sign of a direct confrontation.

The fourth and most significant difference between power and domination involves their respective end results. The end result of power is freedom; that is, I get what I want and then move on to pursue my next objective. The end result of domination is enslavement. To maintain my dominance, I must constantly expend my time and energy to make sure that those whom I am dominating are remaining subservient. For example, when I take my Siberian husky for a walk, there is no question that I have her on one end of the leash. What is just as certain is that she has me on the other end and I have to constantly let her know that I'm in charge.

Another concept frequently confused with power is manipulation. To manipulate is simply to handle; however, with regard to power, it usually carries a more specific and negative meaning. Manipulation can be thought of as the *secret* use of power, implying that another person—who is not fully aware of what is going on—will be used to acquire the objective. It suggests an ulterior motive, withholding information, or using the other person without considering his views or welfare. Power, by contrast, is *open,* does not necessarily involve another person, and presumes no ill will or disregard for others. To illustrate the point, think of the difference between being accused of being powerful and being accused of being manipulative.

Distinctions between power and other concepts such as authority, intimidation, and leadership will be discussed a little later on.

The Nature of Power

Power, an important part of the human condition, has six identifying attributes that give it its unique character:

1. Power is uniquely expressed.
2. Power is a function of individual awareness.
3. There are costs and risks associated with every attempted exercise of power.
4. Power is a neutral force.
5. Power is existential.
6. All power resides in conscious choice.

Power is uniquely expressed. The effective exercise of power lies completely within you and relies on two factors: your ability to pursue the objective and your awareness of how much of that objective is attainable. Your ability to pursue an objective is comprised of all the unique characteristics and personality traits that identify you and distinguish you from every other person. The number of such characteristics is infinite—being aggressive, being logical, being easygoing, being tenacious, being compassionate, and so on. To the extent that you are aware of and value who you are and how you are (as you are), you will be able to express power effectively. The important thing to keep in mind is that there is no single characteristic, or combination of characteristics, that is any better or more effective than any other. All that is required is that you be fully who you are.

Power is a function of individual awareness. To be powerful, that is, to get more of what you want, you must first be aware of what it is that you want. Next, you must be aware of what is going on in the environment around you. And then you have to be aware of how much of what you want is currently available. Regardless of how strong, clear, or positive your approach, if you are lacking in your awareness of any of these three elements, there isn't much chance for success. In fact, not only will the approach fail, but those same characteristics that are so positive when directed effectively will actually be liabilities. Take a kid who wants to stay up an extra half-hour on a school night to see a TV show. Once it is clear that this is not available, any further cajoling, arguing, or wheedling will not only result in frayed nerves and short tempers, but will most likely reduce the kid's chances of getting the next thing asked for.

There are costs and risks associated with every attempted exercise of power. In fact, usually the costs and risks are many and varied, and unavoidable; they simply come with the territory. Assume that you are determined to get a specific project assigned to you and that successful completion of the project will lead to a promotion. Your ability to secure this project would be a clear indication of your power. Note several of the costs/risks that you must face as you proceed:

Risk of failure. If there is an opportunity for success, there is an equal risk of failure. Should you fail, not only do you not get what you wanted, you also weaken your existing track record.

Opportunity cost. By getting this project assigned to you and putting in the time and effort required to make it a success, you must give up the opportunity to pursue other projects that might arise in the meantime. Whenever you say yes to something, you automatically say no to everything else that you might have done at that time.

Risk of rejection. If you are successful, you risk experiencing the displeasure of those who were not successful. As you become more powerful, and as you become comfortable with your power, those who do not feel as good about themselves may love you less. Very few powerful people are universally popular.

Security costs. Each attempted exercise of power, whether or not it is successful, results in a change in the status quo. Nothing is ever exactly the same again. Frequently prestige is lost or gained, track records are altered, and specific wants are met or eliminated, or increased or decreased. What all this means is that each attempted exercise of power entails leaving old, often comfortable, positions and adopting new ones.

Power is a neutral force. By this I mean that in and of itself power is neither good nor bad. Power simply *is!* All too frequently people pursue power for its own sake because they see it as good or they avoid power because they see it as bad. But if anything can be judged as good or bad, it is the objective being pursued, rather than the ability to attain it. Power itself is neutral, and as such it can be approached with much less drama and emotion and can be seen as a force that can be studied, cultivated, and easily controlled as a means of increasing individual and organizational effectiveness.

Power is existential. That is, power can be expressed only right here, right now, at this moment. Your capacity to successfully pursue an objective depends on your ability to stay constantly in touch with conditions as they exist and are changing in the environment. Anything that pushes you into the past, so that you are responding to "what should be happening" instead of to what is actually happening, or into the future, so that you are responding to "what might or might not happen" or so that you are hoping that things will turn out a certain way instead of dealing with conditions as they are, will pull you out of contact with the present and render you ineffective. Similarly, focusing on irrelevant conditions or on relevant conditions that you cannot change right now will have an equally disempowering effect on your getting what you want.

Frequently people who anticipate the future lock themselves into euphoric expectations, "Wow, this is going to be the greatest party ever!" or into catastrophic expectations, "I know that this party is going to be just awful." Once you do this, at either extreme, you are totally out of touch with what is happening in the present and you have little chance of bringing about the desired outcome. One way to counter being caught at one of the extremes is to immediately touch the other extreme. If, for example, you have immobilized yourself by anticipating the worst possible outcome if you ask your boss for a raise, ask yourself, "Realistically, what is the worst thing that could happen to me if I ask?" and then ask yourself, "What is the best thing that could happen to me if I ask?" Touching both extremes will help you to realize that anything is possible. This will allow you to get "centered" in the here-and-now, and you will be able to get moving again.

All power resides in conscious choice. This final attribute is the most important one. It involves the locus of power. The actual choice that you make is secondary; of primary importance is that power is actualized only in the conscious act of choosing.

Furthermore, having only one choice is simply having *no choice.* This is the situation in which you lock yourself into a fixed position, value, or attitude that says that you can respond in only one way, no matter what is occurring or how inappropriate that response might be under the circumstances. Always maintaining a friendly posture regardless of what is going on is one example. When you maintain an "always be . . ." or a "never be . . ." position, you render yourself powerless to choose the most appropriate way for you to react to a particular set of circumstances.

Although still not optimal, two choices are better than one. The problem with a two-choice position, that is, an either/or situation, is that you frequently get caught on the horns of a dilemma—neither choice is ideal, or both choices equally appropriate, and you have no other options. The condition is much like the proverbial donkey that starved to death standing between two equally distant piles of hay.

A very common and disastrous application of the two-choice strategy is giving someone an ultimatum. Suppose you say to Charlie, "Either you complete this project by the end of the week, or I'll see to it that Pete gets the next project!" Once you deliver the ultimatum, the power shifts totally to Charlie, who now is the sole determiner of what you are going to do for the next project.

Even more destructive than this, once you deliver the ultimatum, the situation immediately shifts from goal accomplishment to pure destructive power confrontation. The best possible outcome is that Charlie will give minimal compliance to your ultimatum. This compliance will usually be accompanied by a healthy dose of resentment and a silent vow to get even with you. The worst possible outcome is that Charlie will completely defy you, which will force you either to assume your least preferred position (the "or else") or to back down completely, with a future loss of your credibility. Ultimatums are of value only as a last resort; they should be used only when you have exhausted all other means of getting compliance and you are as ready to go with the or-else alternative as you are with what you wanted initially.

The greater your capacity for generating alternatives, the higher the probability that you will come up with and select the appropriate or effective choice. The minimum number of alternatives necessary for you to fully actualize your power is *three*.

At the beginning of a training program that I conducted recently, I asked a participant what would be the worst possible outcome for him of the three days that we would be together. He said, "To be bored." I asked him what he could do to make sure that boredom didn't set in, and he responded, "I could get up and leave" (choice 1). I said, "Sure you could. What else could you do?" He replied, "I could sit here and turn off" (choice 2). I then said, "Right, but neither of those would get you what you want. What else could you do?" After hesitating for several moments, he grinned and said, "I could shout, '*bored!*' " (choice 3). "Will you do that?" I asked. He said, "Sure." Needless to say, neither of us was bored for the three days.

CHAPTER 2

But First a Little Theory

In taking the view that power is strictly a function of the individual's ability to get what he or she wants from the environment, I need to say a bit about how people go about making, or not making, solid contact with that environment.

Contact

I define *contact* in its simplest form as "the coming together of me with something or someone not me." For example, as I notice the pen in my hand, I'm aware of its color, shape, and size, the smoothness of the plastic, the coolness of the barrel, and so on. The more aspects of the pen that I am aware of, the better the quality of contact that I have with it. That is, the keener my awareness is of its specific attributes, the more I am aware of how it is *literally* different from me. This same process applies to making contact with anything or anyone in the environment. The direct implication of this observation is that *all contact is based on an awareness of differences,* not of similarities. The more that I can distinguish myself from anyone or anything else, the higher the probability that I will be able to appreciate the other for his, her, or its uniqueness and thereby make better contact with that other person or thing.

Let's take a look at an actual example of visual contact. Were I to ask you which of the triangles in Figure 1 is it easier to make contact with, my guess is that you would unhesitatingly choose triangle 3, on the far right.

When you compare triangle 3 with the other two triangles, the characteristics that distinguish it as the most contactful (i.e., the easiest to see and the most clear to understand), are its clarity, its

Figure 1. An example of visual contact.

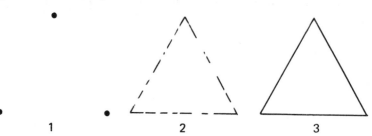

strength, its completeness, its solidity, its definition, and its contrast. These nouns, used to illustrate the contactfulness of a simple triangle, can serve equally well to illustrate the contactfulness of an individual. Thus, a contactful person or thing is one having qualities that make it easy to establish contact with, and a contactful relationship is one in which good contact has been established. I'll be using the word "contactful" to mean both these things throughout the rest of this book.

Boundary

In describing any figure in terms of its shape, we can refer to its boundary. For example, each country on a map is clearly defined and identifiable by its unique boundary. Similarly, triangle 3 in Figure 1 is easily identified by its boundary. As you can readily see, it is made up of three straight lines, each line being a separate and distinct subboundary. These particular lines have no meaning until they are put together to form the triangle.

The I-boundary. Just as triangles have boundaries, so do people. When we refer to people, we do so in terms of the *I-boundary.* The I-boundary consists of all the things that combine to make a person unique and identifiable in this universe. In fact, in terms of contact, the only difference between a person and a triangle is the number of subboundaries it takes to make each one up. A triangle is made up of three subboundaries, a person is made up of hundreds.

First, there are the physical subboundaries—height, weight, length of arm, foot size, and so on. Then there are the psychological subboundaries—attitudes, values, tastes, talents, likes, dislikes, prejudices, and so on. A subboundary, whether physical or psychological, does not address any specific act; rather, it is a *capacity for* something.

For example, I happen to be 5′9″. That is, one physical subboundary that characterizes me is that I start at the floor and go straight up for 5 feet and 9 inches and stop there. Now the truth is that I would love to be 6′4″, but the reality is that I am 5′9″. What this means in terms of effectiveness is that I have the capacity to do most things that someone 5′9″ can do but not all the things that someone 6′4″ can do. Translating this to a practical illustration, in high school I didn't go out for basketball, I went out for wrestling.

The psychological subboundaries operate in exactly the same way, but they define the individual much more than the physical ones do. In viewing the psychological subboundaries, we can say that *all subboundaries cross the continuum at two points between the two polarities*.

All human characteristics can be thought of in terms of *polarities:* love–hate, introvert–extrovert, active–passive, submissive–aggressive, and so on. For the sake of illustration, let's take one continuum that is of general interest both at work and at home—mistrust–trust. In Figure 2 we can view mistrust and trust as extreme opposite positions on a single continuum.

Figure 2. Mistrust–trust continuum.

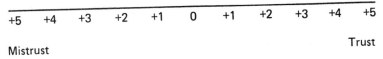

| +5 | +4 | +3 | +2 | +1 | 0 | +1 | +2 | +3 | +4 | +5 |

Mistrust   Trust

In this example, +5 on the left-hand side is as mistrustful as it is humanly possible to be. If I were at this point, I would walk around with a .45-caliber pistol strapped to my hip, a .22 taped to my ankle, and a knife stuck up my sleeve. I would have several locks for each door, which I would change frequently. If I wanted to know if it was raining out, I'd ask three people, independently, and then go outside to make sure that none of them had lied to me.

The polar opposite, +5 on the right-hand side, is as trustful as it is humanly possible to be. If I were at this point, I would believe anything that anybody told me at any time under any circumstances. No matter how many times you had lied to me in the past, I'd still believe you.

But as I mentioned before, all subboundaries cross the continuum at two points between the two polarities and represent a capacity for something. So in Figure 3 my subboundary on the mistrust–trust dimension goes from +2.3 to +3.4.

Figure 3. Mistrust–trust continuum with subboundary indicated.

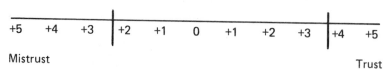

In practical terms, this says that at one extreme I am mistrustful enough never to leave my car unlocked, no matter where I am, and at the other extreme, I am trustful enough to take most people at their word the first time that I meet them. The span of these two positions represents *my* total capacity on the mistrust–trust dimension. No matter where I am or what is going on, if the issue at hand involves some response that pertains to mistrust or trust and I choose to respond within my subboundary, I am likely to be appropriate and effective. That is, my subboundary represents the full range of responses on the mistrust–trust continuum that are appropriate and comfortable for *me*. If the situation is a threatening one, a response from the left side of the scale will be appropriate and in my best interest. If the situation is a supportive one, a response from the right side of the scale will be appropriate.

By knowing where my subboundaries lie, I will always be in a better position to use myself effectively, because it is always the *situation* that determines what response is appropriate.

To illustrate, several years ago my wife and I decided to purchase a new car because our old one was almost completely rusted out. When we took delivery, we decided that it would be smart to invest a few more dollars and get the car rustproofed. When we dropped the new car off—it had to be left overnight—and were ready to drive home in the junker, my wife asked the attendant for a receipt for the car. He smiled, as did I, and he made one out for her on a piece of notebook paper. She then stopped for a moment and asked him to get the serial number off the block and put it on the receipt. He and I both grinned, he got it for her, and we left. On the way home we talked a little about her request, and she rightly pointed out that the car was going to be sitting outside, all night, in a gas station, in a bad part of a town that we didn't even live in. If the car were stolen or severely damaged, we would, at best, have a difficult time proving that it was ours. I, of course, could find nothing wrong with her reasoning; however, I have yet to ask a mechanic or a gas station attendant for a receipt for the car when I drop it off to have work done on it.

Figure 4. The way different subboundaries operate.

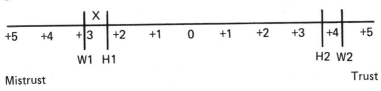

You can see in Figure 4 that at both ends my subboundary (Husband 1–H2) on the mistrust–trust continuum is well within my wife's subboundary (Wife 1–W2). She is more mistrustful than I am, and she also happens to be more trustful than I am. Asking a mechanic for a receipt for a car is an act that comes from point X. It is within her boundary, is comfortable for her, and gets her what she wants, so she does it. It is outside my boundary, and asking for it would make me feel rather foolish and inappropriate, so I don't. This is one of the ways in which we are different!

An individual's I-boundary comprises where he or she falls on all the various subboundaries. For example, in Figure 5, as we start to add

Figure 5. An I-boundary.

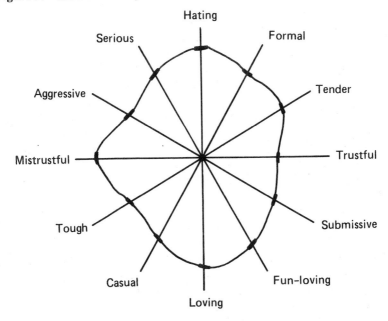

some other subboundaries, you can see that a pattern begins to emerge. The more polarities that are added, the clearer the pattern becomes. In effect, if it were actually possible to physically see your I-boundary, it would look something like the diagram in Figure 5, showing all your subboundaries, that is, where you cross all polarities at two points.

There are two implications of this model that need to be made very explicit. The first is that there is no human characteristic or capacity that is, in and of itself, bad. There is no bad way to be! It is just as valuable and laudable to have a capacity for mistrust as it is to have a capacity for trust, since there are some people out there will treat you fairly and others who, if given the opportunity, will take unfair advantage. It is as necessary to have a capacity for hatred as it is to have a capacity for loving. If I love my son, it is appropriate for me to hate someone who would intentionally harm him.

To forestall any confusion, ways to be are *capacities*. Things such as being a murderer, a psychotic, or a child abuser are *not* ways to be, they are *aberrations* of ways to be. For example, one way to be is to have a capacity for killing. Whereas coldblooded murder is never appropriate, assassinating a vicious tyrant—for example, Adolf Hitler or Idi Amin—might very well be. Likewise, psychosis is an aberration of the capacity to dream, and child abuse is an aberration of the capacity to discipline.

There is no such thing as a bad capacity. Nor are people ever to be judged for their capacities, only for their actions. If you place a high value on human life, you may choose never to kill. It is to your advantage, however, to have the capacity to do so, as just one time it might save your own life or the life of someone you love.

The second implication is that no one has control over his or her I-boundary. That is, you simply are who you are at any given moment. This being the case, the highest payoff seems to come from (1) being fully aware of who you are and how you are and (2) valuing who you are and how you are. No individual has an I-boundary that is remotely like anyone else's. The more you are aware of your uniqueness, and the more you value it, the higher the probability that you will be able to get more of what you want, on the one hand, and that you will be able to make highly valuable contributions, on the other. Right now, at this very moment, you are who you are, with all your likes, dislikes, talents, tastes, preferences, wants, prejudices, and so forth. This is so whether other individuals approve of you or not. It's even so whether *you* approve of you or not. Indeed, the only choice that you have is how you will come across. Referring back to the triangles in Figure 1, will you be practically invisible (No. 1), rather vague (No. 2), or quite clear and distinct (No. 3)? Since your I-boundary is what it is, the more you come across with the clarity of triangle 3, the higher the probability that you will be able to get more of what you want and pay less for it. See Figure 6. As it is with triangles, so it is with people.

The Here-and-Now

The only other thing that needs to be said about contact is that *all contact occurs right here, right now, at this very moment*. Two minutes ago is gone; I can't contact you two minutes ago. Two minutes from now simply doesn't exist yet; it is equally unavailable for contact. Anything that pushes you into the past, such as "should," "ought," or "thou shalt not," is destructive to contact. Similarly, anything that pushes you into the future, such as "what if," "if only," or "I hope," is equally destructive to contact and effectiveness. The more energy that you can focus on what is occurring at the moment, the greater the likelihood that you will be able to make solid contact with the environment and get what you want.

It is important to make a clear distinction between learning *from* the past and being *in* the past. The same distinction needs to be made between *planning* for the future and being *in* the future.

Learning from the past and planning for the future are here-and-now, contactful activities. Being in the past and being in the future are not. For example, if something happens right now and I can make sense out of it by contrasting it with something that I remember, I am learning *in the present*. In addition, this new knowledge becomes a part of my reservoir of knowledge, and I can draw upon it the next time a learning event occurs.

Planning for the future can be viewed in the same way. Suppose that I'm a newly commissioned second lieutenant in the U.S. Army and that I'm firmly committed to a 30-year career. The first thing I do after getting my commission is sit down and get clear about where I want to be at the end of the 30 years. Say that at a minimum I want to retire as a full colonel. Now that I'm clear about that, I can start to plan my career so that I can accomplish my objective on target. The truth is that I want to be a colonel right now, and if I possibly could be I would be, but it's just not possible. All goals, objectives, and plans for them are cast in terms of here-and-now wants. The fact that the learning is occurring right now, as is the wanting, makes both these functions highly contactful. If you stay in the past, longing for things that once were but will never be again, or if you stay in the future, hoping for

Figure 6. Three variants of the I-boundary (from unclear to clear).

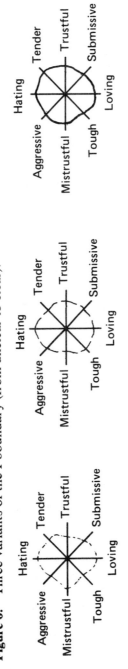

Figure 7. Contact cycle.

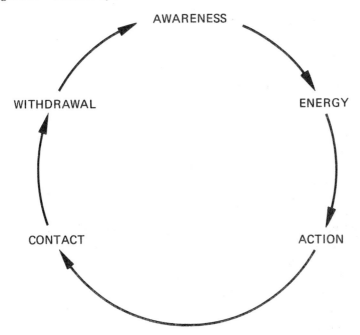

things to change, you can only be disappointed, because you will be unable to have an impact on the present.

To illustrate, take a moment to respond to these two questions: (1) Have you ever in your life had a moment exactly like the one that you are experiencing right now? The answer, obviously, is "Of course not"; you have never read these words on this page for the first time in this context and sequence before. (2) Will you ever again, as long as you live, have a moment exactly like this one? Again, the answer is "Of course not"; you will never again be able to read these words for the *first* time in this context and sequence again. It's true that if you continue to read, two minutes from now will be quite similar to now, in that we will be discussing the same subject. However, the more aware you are of how each moment is *different,* that is, the more you are aware of what you see or experience that you did not see or experience before, the more potent is the moment.

Awareness. Awareness is the most important element in making and maintaining good contact with the environment. The more aware you are of what you feel, value, believe, see, think, want, at any given moment, the easier it is for you to make good contact. Figure 7 illustrates the relationship between awareness and contact; this relationship is known as the *contact cycle.* In the cycle *awareness* leads to *energy,* which leads to *action,* which leads to *contact,* which leads to *withdrawal,* which results in the emergence of a new *awareness.* For example, as I write, I become aware that I am thirsty. This awareness releases energy and directs the action, which is to pick up a glass of water and drink. As the water makes contact with my throat, the thirst lessens. I check to make sure that the thirst is gone, withdrawal, and a new awareness occurs, my need to continue writing.

This cycle starts the moment that you are born, runs nonstop 24 hours a day, and ends the moment you die—and, incidentally, is a large part of what the dream state is about at night, in that the function of dreaming is to increase your awareness of and contact with yourself in areas that are currently hidden or unclear. Often, you begin a quest before you are fully aware of what you want; or you may not be able to marshal all the energy you need; or you may interrupt yourself by starting another quest or focusing on a new awareness before contact is complete on the one in progress. The cycle continues, but it does so in fits, starts, and wobbles, so that closure is rarely complete or fulfilling. One approach to maintaining power is to keep the cycle running as smoothly and uninterruptedly as possible.

Assuming that this view of power and contact is a reasonable one to you, there is an inescapable conclusion that I mentioned earlier and must be repeated here: Since there is no bad way to be, no bad capacity to have, it is always the situation that determines what is appropriate and what is ethical.

Each situation and event in a person's life is unique and cast in circumstances that are forever changing. In one instance, being forceful may be appropriate; 30 seconds later, in a similar but slightly different situation, being pliable may be appropriate. For example, you make a point strongly and forcefully. Someone else listens and responds with a different or opposing view. You listen to her response, gain a new perspective, and from this new perspective see that her suggestion is more appropriate to your getting what you want. You choose to agree, and in that conscious choice you get more of what you want, and at the same time you maintain your power.

Just as the situation always determines what is appropriate, the situation also always determines what is ethical. *Situational ethics* are usually considered to be a manipulative, sleazy, or convenient set of moral standards. I maintain that situational ethics are the only ones that have value. If being appropriate means doing what is effective, then being ethical means doing what is right.

"What is right" refers to an extremely subjective and highly personal set of values. "Doing what is right" refers to actions determined by what is right. And just as there is no action that is in and of itself appropriate or inappropriate, there is also no action that is in and of itself ethical or unethical. To illustrate, most people consider lying to be unethical, and in most cases I would hasten to agree. It is, nevertheless, important to have the capacity to lie. Suppose, to make a really extreme case, that it's 1941 and you are on a train to Berlin. An SS guard comes into the car and asks you directly, "Do you know of any Jewish children on this train?" In fact, you do. Assuming that you are in absolutely no jeopardy yourself no matter how you answer, how would you respond? Or to take a more day-to-day situation, suppose a good friend is excited by a new romance. You meet the "beloved" and are not at all impressed. Later your friend asks, "Wow, isn't she great?" What would you say?

In many situations the choice of which action to take is made between actions that serve competing values. In these illustrations you must choose between the competing values of honesty and not causing pain to others. As long as you make your choice *consciously,* and your choice serves the value that is more important to you, that choice is the ethical one, regardless of which choice you make.

The Doctrine of Separate Boundary

With regard to the direct relationship between contact and power, one very important point needs to be emphasized: *No two people share a common relationship with a third person.* That is, my relationship with any individual stands by itself and has no bearing on any relationship that I have with anyone else.

There is much current theory that runs counter to this view, the most notable probably being Leon Festinger's cognitive dissonance theory. For the sake of illustration, suppose that Pete and Charlie are good friends, and that Pete and Fred are good friends, but that Charlie and Fred can't bear the sight of each other. According to dissonance theory, this condition will cause Pete considerable discomfort and he is likely to put some effort into patching things up between Charlie and Fred in order to reduce his own discomfort. Although most of the time this is the case, it does not have to be this way!

According to my doctrine of separate boundary (DSB), Pete and Charlie's relationship is uniquely theirs, as is Pete and Fred's. What occurs between Charlie and Fred is uniquely theirs, as well. Pete has no responsibility for Charlie and Fred's relationship and no personal stake in its outcome. The essence of DSB is that each individual has responsibility for, and control over, exactly one person in this universe—himself or herself. Many problems that crop up for people in day-to-day work and interpersonal relationships can be attributed to their tendency to feel some responsibility for other people's actions, values, expressiveness, and so on.

The illustration on the left in Figure 8 can be viewed as one of common boundary, with three interacting relationships. The result is a somewhat cloudy situation, with two partially diminished positive relationships and one clearly negative relationship. The configuration on the right is one of separate boundary—there are three separate, unrelated relationships. In this case, the result is two clear and highly positive relationships and one clear, negative one.

Figure 8. Common boundary and separate boundary.

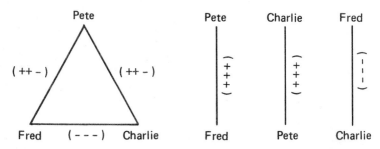

As mentioned, many of the day-to-day interpersonal problems experienced in the home or work setting are due to the individual's inability or unwillingness, first, to take full responsibility for himself or herself and, second, to give up taking responsibility for other people.

A familiar expression of the problem of common boundary involves the issue of personal loyalty, as in "If you like, or support, him, you're no friend of mine!" Individuals who allow themselves to get suckered into buying this position frequently end up with two diminished relationships and a mild to moderate attack of guilt and confusion. Of course, you do not have to buy into this at all. There are three steps involved in breaking out of this debilitating trap:

1. Give yourself permission to like whomever you like for whatever reason that you like him or her.

2. Recognize that you are never under any obligation to justify your preferences to anyone.
3. Recognize that you have responsibility only for what you do, for how you maintain each of your relationships. If Sara dislikes the fact that you have a relationship with Edgar, it is Sara's problem, not yours, unless you choose to let it become yours.

A second "common boundary" problem involves the issue of becoming embarrassed for someone else. Embarrassment for myself usually occurs when I have inadvertently made a complete fool of myself, usually in public, and indicates that I have not lived up to my values or expectations for me. Embarrassment for others occurs when someone else has not lived up to my values or expectations. Being embarrassed for myself can, under certain circumstances, be quite appropriate. Being embarrassed as a result of someone else's actions, however, usually occurs when someone does something that I do not approve of and I react as if that person's experience were happening to me. This is a clear case of common boundary. My disapproval may be appropriate, but not my embarrassment. There have been many times when I have been embarrassed by someone else's actions, only to discover that the person felt fine about himself or herself and that my view of the situation was the minority view among those present.

One way to avoid these feelings of embarrassment and the physical cringe that usually accompanies them is to realize that even though you have every right to set standards for your own behavior, you do not have any right to set standards for the behavior of others. More to the point, you have no responsibility for other people's behavior. From this position I may still heartily disapprove of the act of another person; however, I am not in any emotional discomfort, nor do I cringe. (Note that cringing is a physical act of *self*-protection.)

A third observation in the area of common boundary refers to the phenomenon of jealousy. Of all the forms that common boundary takes, this is probably the most painful and the most destructive.

It would be terribly naive and presumptuous of me to tell anyone not to feel jealous, particularly if the person happens to be right in the middle of feeling jealous. After all, you'll feel what you feel! The major problem is that many people, when they experience jealousy, also feel largely out of control, that is, *victims* of their own feelings or of someone else's actions.

Now let's look at jealousy in terms of separate boundary. Jealousy is the emotional response to not getting all of what you want from another person or to wanting something that is not available from the other person.

Suppose that Tony and Sally have a warm, intimate, reciprocal relationship and that Sally is also somewhat fond of Jerry. When Tony finds out about this, he feels threatened and, of course, jealous. If, however, Tony sits down and gets very clear about what he wants from Sally, and then finds out either that it is available or that he already has it, the relationship between Sally and Jerry becomes much less threatening and much less important.

It is, for me, quite reasonable to want to be the most important person in someone else's life. It is totally unreasonable for me to expect to be the *only* person in someone else's life. If you set your expectations in terms of what you consider reasonable and potentially available, you can avoid most jealousy.

If each relationship is freely established and *agreed upon* in terms of what both parties want and do not want from each other, there is much less chance that jealousy will enter into it, and both parties will be able to move freely within the parameters of the relationship without causing undue pain to each other or guilt to themselves.

To illustrate, some years back I was conducting a program and one of the participants expressed a desire to get closer to me. This did not fit for me at the time, so I said, "I don't feel the need to get closer at this point, but neither do I feel any need to move farther away. Is this okay for you for right now?" She hesitated for a moment, then smiled and said yes. Later it did fit for me, and today she is a very close friend of our family.

If you approach any relationship in terms of mutual wants and agreements, the probability is very high that some very positive things will be available, even if everything that you originally wanted is not. For example, being told, "I am giving the promotion to Susan; however, I am pleased with your work and want you to know that if you continue to progress, you will be in line shortly," is not as good as getting the promotion. But it will go a long way toward reducing the resentment and jealousy you might otherwise feel, and it will allow you to focus your energy on what you need to do to get the next promotion and to do it from a position of feeling appreciated rather than from a position of feeling rejected.

There is a path for dealing with jealousy productively that, although risky, can help reduce jealousy.

1. Keep in mind that jealousy is something that *you do to you*, not something that the other person does to you.

2. Get clear about what *you* want from the other person for *you*. This may not include a demand concerning a third party.
3. See how much of what you want is available. (There may be, and frequently is, enough for right now.)

Awareness and the skillful use of contact are the most important tools needed to express power. Contact has been discussed primarily in the context of communicating with other people. Contact can be made by taking a moment to be aware of yourself; then, aware of the others; and finally, aware of the unique moment in time in which the particular situation takes place.

It is important to emphasize that although we traditionally think of contact as a function of interpersonal communication, it is hardly restricted to that. Whether I am playing with my dog, listening to a favorite piece of music, or designing a new workshop, getting the most out of each situation is going to be contingent upon my ability to make and maintain effective contact.

CHAPTER 3

Power Lost

A major contention of this book is that power is a natural state. *No one has to be taught how to be powerful.* Take a look at any child under the age of 6 if you want to see proof of this. Kids make their demands clearly; they know what they want at any given moment; they do not collude with adults who are not giving them what they want; they are the world's sorest losers; and I have yet to see a kid go along with that rationalization, "I'm only doing this to you for your own good." Above all, kids will take various tacks in pursuit of an objective. If asking doesn't work, they'll try wheedling. If wheedling doesn't work, they'll try a tantrum. They'll continue this until they are either successful or finally and totally blocked.

Methods of Disempowerment

Since power is natural, the question arises: how come so many people see themselves, and are seen by others, as being powerless? The obvious answer to this question is that powerlessness is carefully taught and is just as carefully learned.

One more point before we turn to a discussion of some of the ways in which power is lost: *Nobody has the capacity to empower or disempower any other individual.* If, for whatever reason, you submit to my will without consciously choosing to do so, you do not make me more powerful, you simply make yourself less so. If, on the other hand, you comply with my wish by your own choice, you have lost no power and you have not affected my power in one way or the other. In many instances, individuals disempower themselves, not so much because they fear the risks associated with using power, but because they are not aware that they are disempowering themselves. Several of the more common ways in which people disempower themselves are discussed here.

Overemphasizing Credentials

One of the most common and least obvious ways that people disempower themselves is by responding inappropriately to other people's credentials. Credentials take many forms—academic degrees, organizational rank, real or implied experience, and status, to name just a few. Regardless of the type or quality of the credential, the moment that you allow the so-called expert to make the choice, you thoroughly disempower yourself.

Used judiciously, other people's credentials are an important and valuable resource to individuals and organizations. A person's credentials say, in effect, "Listen to what I have to say." They do not say, "Do what I think is best for you." The trick to effectively utilizing people's credentials is to listen carefully to what these people have to say and then to consciously choose to agree, disagree, or modify the expert opinion to your specific need. The credentialled person's function is to supply the information, viewpoint, or value. This is the contribution that is made by consultants, counselors, and analysts. It is your function, and responsibility, to make the decision. And as long as you make the decision, you are powerful, regardless of what the decision is or of who suggested it initially.

There are two reasons why this form of disempowerment is so seductive. First, people frequently forget that their ability to reason and think is *at least* as powerful as another person's credentials and experience. By allowing themselves to become overly focused on, or awed by, another's credentials, their awareness of their own strength is lost. Second, you are the world's foremost authority on yourself! No one knows better than you what is best for you. No one has had your experience, is more concerned for your welfare, or knows more about what you want than you. In fact, no one else even comes close. The expert, while knowing much more about his or her area of expertise than you do, knows much less than you do about how this knowledge will affect, benefit, or threaten you personally. In contrast with the notion that knowledge is power, I think that decision is power.

Unclear Wants

A major reason that many people don't have the power to get what they want is that they don't know what they want. The knowledge is there; they are simply unaware of it.

You are responsible at all times for everything you do or don't do and for everything you say or don't say. There are, however, two areas for which no one is accountable to anyone else, living or dead, under any circumstance; these are: what you feel and what you want.

You are going to feel what you feel and want what you want regardless of who approves or disapproves. Moreover, you are a lot more effective when you allow these processes to occur naturally than when you attempt to block or suppress them. By allowing yourself to surface the wants clearly, you gain in two ways. First, the more quickly and clearly you acknowledge the want, the easier it is for you to develop and pursue a strategy to attain it. Second, if the want surfaces clearly and is not attainable at this time, it is much easier for you to set it aside temporarily and get in touch with a secondary want that is attainable right now.

One way that you may have been stopped from developing clear wants is that you were told by other people, "You shouldn't want that!" Usually this occurs as a part of child rearing and is done with the very best intentions on the part of the parent, teacher, or religious leader. Regardless of how good the intentions are, this experience has several disastrous and inevitable results.

The first, and most immediate, result is that you think of yourself as evil, weak, or unworthy of love or respect for *wanting* something. This is hardly supportive of your developing into a strong, powerful adult.

The second result is even more damaging, if that is possible. Children, as well as adults, learn very quickly how to get what they need. If approval of the other person is critical to you, you will learn how to get it. The confounding factor here is that if you are successful in obtaining approval, what you will have learned is not to stop wanting something but, rather, how to *not be aware* of wanting something. The upshot is that the other person has effectively cut you off from a living part of yourself. Your wants are an intrinsic part of your I-boundary, which defines and identifies you and differentiates you from others, and you have every right to know about and make use of every aspect of your I-boundary.

The third result is that you get used to this situation and see it as okay and natural. It may be marginally acceptable for you as a youngster to come to your father and ask, "Daddy, is it okay for me to want this?" (A wise parent will sit down with you and use the opportunity to discuss the pros and cons of getting this thing.) It's an altogether different matter when you ask the same question 30 years later. When people attempt to control your wants, they are at the same time forcing, and then reinforcing, a subtle and permanent state of dependence in you, so that you will always feel the need to go to someone else to check out whether it's okay for you to want the promotion, the car, the divorce, or whatever.

Note that being told what you should want is no better than being told what you shouldn't want. The same goes for being told how or what you should or shouldn't feel, think, prefer, see, support, and so on. The more a "should" is imposed on you, the less likely you will be to use your own resources to get what you wanted. It's infinitely better if someone works with you to help you to get clear about what it is you want and about the effects of getting it than it is for someone to "teach" you what you should want.

One way that people stop themselves from forming clear, attainable wants is by casting their wants in general, rather than specific terms. Suppose that when asked what you want, you say, "I want to be happy." This is all right in and out of itself, but if left there, nothing of value will happen. Happiness is a feeling, not an objective. What you need here is a clear and specific statement about what would have to happen for you to feel happy. If you were asked directly, "What would it take to make you happy?" and you answered, "Getting the promotion," your want would be clear and you could then determine its attainability. If you get the promotion, the resulting feeling that you have is happiness. Many people spend inordinate amounts of time fully experiencing their unhappiness without ever realizing that they are condemning themselves to this state by not focusing on the specific elements, or lack of them, that are producing the undesired feeling.

A third major source of disempowerment through unclear wants is being unclear about the attainability of what you want. I mentioned attainability in my definition of power. Here I'm focusing on the most universally wanted/least attainable thing of all—change in other people. (This want is especially debilitating when you direct it toward yourself.) You often hear statements in the work setting like "I really wish Charlene were easier to get along with" or "I'd like Morty to show more initiative around here." It is as unlikely that you will get someone, yourself included, to change a personality characteristic as it is that you will get the person to change his or her eye color. By being specific in your demands on others, you focus on their behavior, not on their personalities. You are more likely to get what you want by saying, "Charlene, I'd appreciate it if you'd at least grunt when I say good morning," or "Morty, I want you to be here on time every morning from now on," than you are if you cast your demand in terms of the person's changing who or how he or she is.

There is also a major risk in asking people to change that very few individuals are aware of. If you ask the person to change and you are successful, you're stuck with what you've got. If you think back to how the I-boundary is made up of all the subboundaries, then what you have to keep in mind is that a change in any subboundary will change the entire shape of the I-boundary. You might be really happy with the change that the other person makes for you but not be so happy with how this change affects your overall experience of him or her. Suppose you are constantly on your child for being silly, and he finally succumbs to your view that silliness is bad and then decides to never be silly again. Along with the silliness goes playfulness and probably some humor. Be careful about what you want, you might end up getting it!

The Fallback. It may happen that you will know exactly what you want, and you will be firmly committed to attaining it, only to discover, midway in the pursuit, that it is not completely available to you. This situation is sometimes unavoidable since you can only estimate how much of what you want is available to you before pursuing it. Once engaged in the pursuit, you uncover new information which tells you how you are doing. Sometimes the message of the new information is: "Sorry, you can't have it all this time." Because you know this will happen from time to time, develop a fall-back position once you are clear about what constitutes all of what you want. I am not, for one moment, suggesting that you assume a compromise position! But it is wise to recognize that you can't always know what's available to you until you try to attain it. Once you have given it your best shot and have discovered that all of what you want isn't available, you can shift your position to comply with the conditions as they exist, and paradoxically, still continue your pursuit of "all that is available" even though, realistically, your expectations have been curtailed downward.

For example, suppose that you were in line to direct a project, only to find out that part of it might be allocated to another department. Making a clear pitch for the whole thing is still the way to go. However, if, in the process, you find out that the decision to give away part of it has already been made, you will be in a position to react quickly to that information and take what is there. Being a director is best, but being a co-director is a lot better than not being director at all.

Being aware that there is a fall-back position represents the third position necessary to express power. The first position is to get all of what you initially wanted. The second position is to get none of what you originally wanted. The third position, the fall-back, is to pursue what is available. Do not confuse fall-back positions with compromise. To compromise, you have to give up something that is important to you in order to get what you want. Compromise usually implies settling for less than what is available. In the fall-back position, there is no compromise, since what you originally wanted is not available, and you can't give up something that you never had.

Let me recall an incident that illustrates what happens if you don't take the time to develop a fall-back position. When my wife Jeri and I, once again, needed a new car, we looked around and test-drove various models and decided on what we wanted. I checked the car out in various consumer publications and found out the exact markup on the car we wanted. We went back to the showroom one evening to start the buying ritual. After talking with our salesman for a bit about the car, we got to the critical point. It was now 9:00 p.m., Jeri had a bad cold, and I was tired and a little cranky. The salesman made the traditional opening gambit by saying, "Make an offer." Jeri and I half-heartedly talked it over for about 15 seconds and I gave him a figure. He said, "I'll be right back," and took the figure to the sales manager. He came back smiling and said, "We accept. Congratulations." Unless this has happened to you, you have no idea how painful it is to have a car salesman accept your first offer!

I had screwed up in two ways. First, I wanted to be fair to the salesman, as if he couldn't take of himself. The second way I screwed up was in not putting forth a price that I would like to pay, and then offering a fall-back price that I was willing to pay, and not go one penny above that.

The value of having a clear fall-back position applies to any aspect of power, because without it you are needlessly vulnerable. The salesperson who has only one major account or the consultant who has only one major client is at the mercy of those whom he is trying to serve. In that situation, the tendency is to be self-protective, rather than effective. In personal relationships, the level of intimacy that you would like might not be available, however, there may be enough to give you what you need at the moment.

Confluence

The number one killer of individual power and organizational effectiveness today is *confluence*. In the physical sense the word means "a running together" and usually refers to the area where two streams run together to form a third stream. For example, the Golden Triangle in Pittsburgh is where the Allegheny and the Monongahela

Rivers come together to form the Ohio River. Upstream the water is clearly identifiable as Allegheny or Monongahela, and downstream the water is clearly identifiable as Ohio, but at the area of confluence, where they all come together, you can't tell which water belongs to what river. This idea can be applied to people also.

In families and organizations, confluence occurs when individual identify is sacrificed for the common identity, norms, and values. This results in a blurring of boundaries and a diminishing of individual and unique inputs. Confluence also occurs on a one-to-one basis, when one person wants to be more like another person, the most extreme example being hero worship. Confluence occurs whenever what you see or want or think or value is less important to you than what someone else sees or wants or thinks or values. When this occurs, you are making a psychological merge of your boundary with the other person's, and in that act you become confluent with him or her. As contact is the principal path to power, so confluence is the principal means by which power is lost.

The *perceived* benefits of confluence are feelings of security, togetherness, belonging, harmony, and calm. The costs are loss of power, reduced self-awareness, individual and group ineffectiveness, low energy, low creativity, low risk taking, and superficial relationships.

The positive views of confluence seem to have originated as part of the human relations movement, on the assumption that good work comes out of good working relationships. If this is the major assumption, then clearly the way to produce good work is to develop good working relationships. The result of learning to get along better, to trust, share, and cooperate, will be higher output, more productivity, and happier workers. I hasten to point out that there is nothing wrong with these objectives and that good working relationships are important. The problem here is that in a confluent system, the only working relationships that are considered good are of the warm, supportive variety. Statements of anger, disagreement, and self-interest are discouraged, because they tend to disrupt the warm, cushy "we" feeling that the organization and its members have spent time, energy, and organizational resources developing. Confluence, achieved and striven for, can be recognized in an organization by such statements as "We're just one big happy family" and "What we need around here is more teamwork," when the work itself does not dictate the need for teamwork at all. Other signs of confluence are agreeing too quickly, never disagreeing with certain individuals, and an unusual amount of horseplay and friendly zapping (sarcasm) in the absence of clear disagreement. Another symptom that I became aware of in working with confluent systems is that the members seem to genuinely like each other and to play together very well. The problem is that they don't work together very well and there is relatively low creativity and risk taking as compared to contactful systems. The problem is further compounded and reinforced because top management has been told by highly paid experts that this is the best way to run an organization. What is experienced as a team in a confluent system is identified as a love puddle in a contactful system.

There is an alternative approach to consider. The approach just discussed is based on the premise that good work comes out of good working relationships. The alternative premise is: Good working relationships come out of doing good work together. The distinction is by no means a semantic one. It's a matter of what is the cart and what is the horse. If you espouse the first view, that good work comes out of good working relationships, what you do is focus on the relationships, as just described, and when they are good, the result will be good work. If you espouse the second view, that good working relationships come out of doing good work together, what you do is focus on the work—high performance standards, challenging work, increased responsibility—and the result of meaningful and important accomplishment with co-workers will be stronger, more productive working relationships.

In the confluent approach, the group norm is: "In this organization we learn to like, appreciate, and trust each other." In the contactful approach, the group norm is: "In this organization, you are free to be fully who you are and how you are, and I'm free to like it or not like it. And I am free to be fully who I am and how I am, and you're free to like that or not like that." Frankly, having used both sets of assumptions, I have found that the second is less complex and a lot easier to work from and a damn good way for adults to work together. (Interestingly, kids don't know any other way to work together—until they are taught differently by adults.)

If you want to do a quick check on which approach is preferable, think about the last time that the *situation* really demanded that you get along well, for example, the boss was over for dinner or your mother-in-law was visiting for two weeks. Do you remember the tremendous amount of energy it took for you to keep the smile on your face, to laugh at the right times, and to hold back the anger or disagreement when you felt it? If you can relate to this, you are aware that the enormous amount of energy that it takes to get along well when you don't want to get along well is energy that is not getting put into the work.

Confluence is every bit as dysfunctional to family and personal relationships as it is to working relationships. Signs that it is occurring in the family are statements like "You catch more flies with sugar than you do with vinegar" and "If you can't say something nice, don't say anything at all." Confluence occurs in interpersonal relationships whenever the other person's approval of you is more important to you than your approval of you.

Some years back an amusing incident really heightened my awareness of the characteristics of confluence in families. On a cold, wet Saturday afternoon when my son, who was about 8 years old at the time, and I were watching reruns on TV, a particularly placid episode of *Father Knows Best*, with the Anderson family, was followed immediately by a rather volatile episode of *All in the Family*, with the Bunkers. When the second show was over, I casually asked Eric, "If you couldn't live with Mom and me and you had to pick between the Andersons and the Bunkers, which family would you choose?" With no hesitation he said emphatically, "The Bunkers." The quickness and strength of his response surprised me a little until I thought about it. The Bunkers were alive! They fought together, supported and attacked each other, were silly, serious, and almost every other way there is for people to be with each other. Life with the Andersons, at least in this episode, was an unending excursion into calmness and perpetual understanding, and for me and my kid at least it would be like being a galley slave on the good ship Lollipop.

If you discover that you are being confluent with someone else, and my guess is that most people will find this happening from time to time, there is something that you can do to stop it. List five things about the other person that you really like or admire, and five things that you do not like or admire. Then list five things that you are better at than the other person.

Incidentally, if you find that someone is attempting to be confluent with you, encourage that person to go through the same process. You're a lot better off with a strong friend or supporter than you are with a sycophant.

Self-Intimidation

One of the more fearsome forms of disempowerment is self-intimidation. Not only is this form very painful, but each time that it occurs, the probability that it will occur again increases. Self-intimidation occurs each time you say about someone else, "She scares the hell out of me!"

The most confounding aspect of self-intimidation is that it is based entirely on myth. *Nobody has the power to intimidate anybody else.* When you feel intimidated by someone else, what is actually occurring is that you are not owning up to or taking responsibility for your own intimidation, and in weakening yourself, you are making the other person seem awesome. As stated earlier, you are responsible for exactly one person in this universe—yourself! By recognizing this and taking complete responsibility for your own reactions to other people and events, you gain more control. If you experience yourself as being intimidated by someone else and you take full responsibility for this reaction, you see yourself as being *situationally* powerless, which is something that you can change, rather than seeing the other person as being more powerful, which is something that you cannot change.

Intimidation is usually a function of silently comparing yourself with someone else, then deciding that the other person has won; you have lost a race that was never run. Frequently intimidation starts as an honest and accurate appreciation or respect for another person's physical appearance or other characteristics. The process of disempowerment through intimidation begins when you lose your awareness of your own strength by overfocusing on the other person's strength.

A simple way to check this process is to ask yourself, "What's the worst thing that this person could really do to me if I disagreed with or disapproved of what she said?" More times than not, the honest reply to this question will boil down to "Get angry with me," "Yell at me," or "Not like me as much anymore," none of which, I hasten to point out, is terminal.

Self-intimidation reduces your power not only in situations with a potential for conflict but also in situations with a potential for intimacy. How often have you heard someone say or said to yourself, "Wow, is she something else! I could never handle that!" By the way, the statement "He turns me on" is just as disempowering as "He scares the hell out of me." The fact is that *I* turn me on and then target it on the other person. By taking full responsibility for my own sexuality, as with my own strength, I have more control in each situation. The bottom line is: You're only outclassed if you think you're outclassed!

A lot has been written in the past few years about how to intimidate other people. Most of it centers on how to dress, decorate an office, order wines, buy cars, and so forth. There is even one story circulating about a very powerful naval admiral who was very short. It was said that he ordered that the bottom of the legs of the guest chairs in his office be sawed off. That way his visitors would have to look up to him while they conversed.

I think that this approach to being powerful is a little silly. I am sure that it is effective in some cases, or the power brokers wouldn't be advocating it so strongly. The point is that since nobody can disempower you, it works only if you let it work, only if you respond to the symbols the way they tell you to respond to them. (Remember, as they tell you how to intimidate others by dressing a certain way, they are at the same time giving you the criterion by which you are supposed to be intimidated.)

Clearly, you can choose to see a Saville Row suit as a field marshal's uniform, or you can choose to see it as a really nice set of threads. Only you can turn the boss's office into a throne room, or transform the boardroom into a sanctuary. Again, keep in mind that they can lay the traps and you can choose not to fall into them.

Let me illustrate the way the concept of self-intimidation works by briefly recounting an unfortunate episode that occurred a little over a year ago.

The wife of a close friend of mine owns a children's gift shop in a small shopping center near the local university. There had been a series of armed robberies by a man armed with a hunting knife. His method was to wait until one of the shops was empty except for a lone female employee. He would then enter the shop, rob and sometimes beat the woman, and then escape on foot, losing himself in the crowds of students. He had knocked over six stores up to this point, and his description was known.

Lori's store was number seven. He entered the shop, she recognized him, and before he could say or do anything, she sprayed him with mace from a canister that she always kept with her. But the mace can was defective, and instead of disabling the robber, she only made him angry. He knocked her to the floor, kicked her a few times, robbed the store, and took off. Fortunately for her the man was wearing sneakers, so she escaped with a few bruises and a bad shaking up. When the man was finally caught and tried, he was sentenced to 30 years to life.

We were discussing the event recently, and Lori said to me, "He really intimidated me and I was totally powerless." My response to her was, "Wrong on both counts!" I was able to get her to see that several separate events had actually occurred. The first event was that the robber entered the store and she *chose* to attack first. The attack failed, he counterattacked, and she *chose* to be totally passive, which under the circumstances was exactly the right response. Not only was she not powerless all through this incident, she was in fact extremely powerful. What she experienced was really not intimidation, but fear, which is a very functional capacity to have, since it alerts you to a clear and present danger in the environment. Had she really been powerless, she would have been out of control and might have tried to attack again or might have panicked and screamed uncontrollably, either of which could have had a disastrous outcome.

I must underscore the point that often you have very little, if any, control over what occurs in the environment. However, you always have total control over how you choose to respond to what occurs. This ability to choose your response is power.

Responding Too Quickly

Conscious choosing requires time—time to generate alternatives and time to choose among them. You are robbed of this time every time you place another person's need for a response above your own need for time to weigh the alternatives and choose an appropriate response.

Often when another person makes a demand on you, you automatically go into a state of urgency whether or not such a state actually exists. Frequently the result is a hastily made commitment that you later regret, halfhearted compliance based on guilt, or an equally halfhearted attempt to get out of a commitment because you made the promise too quickly.

Remember: Even though the other person always has the right to ask or demand, you always have the right to agree, disagree, or make a counteroffer. It is essential, and beneficial to both parties, that you take the time to respond accurately, so that you get what you want and the other person can rely on your response. An incident comes to mind. In a recent group session one participant was agonizing over the fact that a close friend had asked him to participate in a race, as a team member. Honored at being asked, he quickly responded that he would be delighted to participate, only to realize a short time later that he really didn't want to. Running would mean that he would have to curtail his usual Saturday night activities because he would have to get up very early on Sunday to compete. He spent three full days agonizing over this situation. If he ran, he would be missing something more important to him than running; if he didn't run, he would feel guilty and be considered unreliable by the other team members. Obviously, the whole thing could have been avoided had he simply said, "Thanks for asking me. Let me think about it and get back to you."

Sometimes the situation dictates that all the time you want or need is not available. Whether it is or not, you're still stuck with whatever you commit to freely. Probably the biggest trap lies in the statement, "Boy, have I got a terrific deal for you, but I've got to have an answer right away." Assuming no ill intent on anyone's part, I have neverthe-less learned to walk away from most offers that are presented in this way.

An interesting variation of this is what I have come to think of as "the tyranny of the telephone." I would probably bodily eject anyone who burst uninvited into my office or home and interrupted what I was doing. But I extend every courtesy to the same person who does this by telephone. I also have a much greater tendency to say yes on the telephone than I do when I am dealing with someone face to face. I don't understand why this happens, but I accept that it does, and I have found a phrase that helps me in these circumstances—"Let me get back to you"—that is, when I remember to use it.

Fear of the Unknown

The proverb Better the devils we have than those we know not of is probably as good a way as any to say that people find it difficult to function in ambiguity.

The tendency, for many people, is to sit safely and securely in one location and to frighten themselves into immobility by fantasizing about what *might* happen. As mentioned earlier, we have control only over reactions to events that are occurring in the present. Often, anticipating possible negative outcomes for any future event is produc-tive and a good way to avoid potentially disastrous results. But it is quite a different thing to anticipate a negative outcome and then react as if it were guaranteed to happen.

Often, the problem is that people will not give themselves permis-sion *not to know* something when that is the situation. The result is that when there is an absence of information, worry rushes in to fill the vacuum and renders the person powerless.

The best way to check this is to recognize that you do not know what is going to happen and to then refocus your attention on what is occurring in the present. Failing this option—if anticipation is unavoid-able—try fantasizing the opposite outcome from the one you fear. For example, if you have just inadvertently insulted your boss's intelli-gence, try working on the assumption that maybe you *won't* get fired, rather than on the one that maybe you will. Although neither assump-tion will have any effect whatsoever on the outcome, using this method will save you a little wear and tear on your stomach lining and keep you more focused in the present. For example, if my family is late in getting home and I'm there waiting for them, my statement to me is, "Maybe they're *not* dead in a ditch."

If you are bound and determined to worry in spite of everything else, at least take the time to fully recognize it for what it is: a nonproductive, freely chosen journey into self-torture. And then do it fully and completely, and have done with it! In a training program that I recently conducted, I asked, "What's the best thing that could happen for you here, in these two days?" One participant, Stan, replied, "Help me to stop worrying." I said, "Okay, I have a homework assignment for you. What I want you to do is set aside a large amount of time tonight for worrying. Be by yourself and take all the time you need. Keep a pad and pencil with you and write down everything that you worry about. I want you to start by saying out loud, 'Now I am going to start worrying.' When you are finished, I want you to say, 'Now I am going to stop worrying.' Whenever you decide to worry I want you to use these two phrases to bracket the time."

The next morning, we were all interested in finding out how it went for Stan. It turned out that Stan had initially set aside one hour to worry, had ended up worrying for exactly twelve minutes, and that was it for the night. Telling yourself, "I shouldn't worry," is no more effective than someone else telling you that you shouldn't worry. If you are going to worry, make it a conscious choice and then stay in control of the process. I can't promise that it will work for you, but it sure worked for Stan.

Fear of Rejection

There is no question that rejection is often painful. There is also no question that painful as it is at times, rejection isn't terminal. No one has ever died from rejection! When I say that nobody has ever died from rejection, I am being quite literal. There are countless movie, TV, and literary plots that center on rejected lovers killing themselves, each other, or anybody else that they can manage to get lined up in the cross hairs of their gunsights. It happens in fiction, and it also happens in real life. What is occurring here is that the individual cannot cope appropriately with *pain*, regardless of its source, and so he responds to it inappropriately through the aberrant behavior of killing. The source of the pain is of secondary, or no, importance. If the person's response to intense pain is to kill someone, it is just as possible for the source of that pain to be career failure, physical injury, having been cheated, or financial despair as it is for it to be rejection. Let me restate it for emphasis: **If somebody you care about rejects you, regardless of the pain you may experience at the time, you're not going to die!**

In many situations—organizational and interpersonal—people fail to pursue their objectives because they fear they will be rejected in the process. Often, this fear of rejection looms larger than the risk at hand. The longer the risk you wish to avoid stays hidden and unknown, the more frightening it is likely to become.

The whole subject of rejection and its consequences needs to be taken out of the closet and aired, if only to reduce some of the unwarranted fear that is often associated with it. Rejection can be broken down into five major categories: fantasied, projected, introjected, boundary fusion, and authentic.

Fantasied rejection. Fantasied rejection usually occurs in the early stages of a relationship when one individual perceives a rejection when in fact no rejection has occurred. For example, suppose that Jason, a newly appointed supervisor, greets his new boss, Linda, with a warm, cheery, "Good morning." Linda looks up, nods, and keeps on walking. The tendency for Jason is to perceive a rejection by Linda and go immediately into a state of low-grade pain.

The reality, of course, is that no rejection has occurred in this brief interchange, only a disparity in expressiveness. Linda's lack of enthusiasm could be attributed to any number of causes, such as preoccupation with work, an upset stomach, or maybe even a feeling of having been rejected by someone else.

The real problem with fantasied rejection is that it generates unnecessary defensive feelings, which in turn produce behaviors that inhibit important relationships or prevent them from developing. Once a *perception* of rejection has occurred, and the pain has been experienced, the tendency is now to avoid the other person, for fear of more pain from more rejection. The outcome of fantasied rejection is that power is lost because of the unwillingness to contact another person. Fantasied rejection also often leads directly to the second form of rejection, that is, projected rejection.

To stop fantasied rejection, you must check out your perception with the other individual at a later time. Even if you find out that you were right, that you were, in fact, rejected, you're no worse off than before you checked it out. Were Jason to approach Linda at a later time and say, "You seemed distant this morning. Are you sore at me for something?" he would immediately be in a position to deal effectively with the situation, one way or the other, thus regaining his power.

Projected rejection. Projection is a condition that exists when you unconsciously attribute your feelings to another person. The question "Why is he angry with me?" can often be more accurately stated as "Why am I angry with him?" Feelings of rejection, just as any other feelings, can be inappropriately projected onto other people. In this, you who are feeling the pain of rejection are, in fact, the one who has actually rejected the other person.

A rather dramatic example of this occurred several years ago in a group with which I was working. Margaret became very upset over the fact that she had been rejected by her sister. Both Margaret and Sara had been raised and educated under very strict, fundamentalist religious principles. Upon reaching adulthood, Margaret informed Sara that she was leaving the small fundamentalist college that they were both attending, as well as the life style in general, and striking out on her own. Sara's immediate response was that she wanted no more to do with Margaret, and she proceeded to resist all of Margaret's attempts at contact from that point forward. Although at first glance it looks as if Sara rejected Margaret, in reality Margaret was the rejector. By initially rejecting the values and mores Sara held so dear, Margaret rejected Sara. Sara perceived the rejection as a personal one, and responded as the injured party with counterrejection. In the incident between Jason and Linda, had Jason's response to Linda's nod been, "Well, to hell with her too!" Jason would have been the rejector, not Linda. In projected rejection, power is lost by not recognizing and taking responsibility for one's legitimate role as a rejector.

Introjected rejection. In Gestalt terminology, *introject* means "to swallow whole." In the physical sense, food introjected or swallowed whole is food ingested without being chewed. This usually results in the food being passed through or ejected without any nourishment being taken from it. This is usually experienced as nausea, indigestion, or other gastrointestinal discomfort.

In the psychological sense, introjection occurs in much the same way and is one of the most damaging forms of confluence. Introjection occurs psychologically when you adopt a position or a value without ever examining (chewing) it, because it is espoused by someone else. (The "shoulds/should nots" discussed earlier are introjects.)

Introjected rejection is the most damaging form of rejection to the individual and is also both the most acutely and the most chronically painful. It usually occurs in established relationships and is a reaction to a *real* rejection by someone else. What makes this so destructive is that when you reject me, *I* reject me at the same time. That is, I swallow your rejection of me, and I reject myself; since I am unworthy and undesirable in your eyes, I become unworthy and undesirable in my own.

Suppose, in response to Jason's question "You seemed distant this morning. Are you sore at me for something?" Linda says, "Look,

Jason, we'll work together as the job dictates, but frankly I don't like you very much, and I don't think too much of your ideas.'' If Jason discounts his own personality, or values his position less, *solely* because Linda disapproves, he diminishes himself and must take full responsibility for the power that he loses by internalizing Linda's disapproval.

Boundary fusion. A disastrous form of rejection often occurs through boundary fusion, that is, not taking the time or having the awareness to distinguish the *act* from the *person* performing the act. In many such cases of perceived rejection, a specific event or act is being rejected without ever implying rejection of the individual. For example, Jack says to his mother, "The meat is a little tough tonight Mom," and she replies tearfully, "You don't love me anymore!" An example between spouses might be: "If you loved me, you'd take out the garbage without my having to ask you every single time!" The reality is that one has absolutely nothing to do with the other. It is very important to personalize things that are personal; it is equally important not to personalize things that are not. Boundary fusion occurs just as frequently in the work setting as in the home setting, with equally disastrous results, as when your proposal is rejected and you put yourself in the dumper right along with it.

There are rare occasions when simultaneous rejection of an event and an individual can occur. It is important to realize, however, that even under such conditions, these are still two separate, although related, events that may or may not occur together. For example, you catch someone whom you have trusted implicitly in the act of stealing from you. You reject the act, and because you consider the act unforgivable, you also reject and say goodbye to the person.

In boundary fusion, power is lost when you are unable to distinguish between the rejection of a specific behavior and the rejection of you as a whole person.

Authentic rejection. Although quite painful at times, authentic rejection is the only form of rejection that heals cleanly and does not involve a loss of power. Authentic rejection occurs when your advances are rejected or your relationship with another person is unilaterally ended by the other person with a simple, "Goodbye." In these instances, no rejection of yourself or loss of self-esteem need occur. It is simply necessary for you to realize that there is no availability for a relationship or that the time for this relationship is over. You need to honor this fact and to end the relationship cleanly. Although there is no denying your pain, it is the legitimate pain of sadness that occurs when a relationship ends. It does hurt, but the hurting does end, so that you can pursue new and different relationships wholly and productively.

Often when you experience rejection, it is unworkable in a practical sense, because you experience it as something to be avoided, or if you cannot avoid it, then you must suffer over it. The trick here is to view rejection as a *natural risk* in all relationships and not as any kind of statement about your worth as a person.

Not getting the promotion, not getting accepted into the graduate program, failing to get the party's nomination, or not being included on *the* mailing list—all have as much potential for producing feelings of rejection as does rejection in the intimate or personal relationship. When dealt with authentically, rejection implies *no* loss of power!

Needing Guarantees

Two aspects of power mentioned earlier involved its existential nature and the fact that you have little, if any, control over events occurring in the environment, only over your reactions to them. A common form of disempowerment occurs when you ignore these elements and ask for, or demand, guarantees from others.

Guarantees are rarely available in terms of outcomes and are never available in terms of personality or attitude change. Guarantees are also, by definition, cast into the future and do not take into consideration all the changes that can occur from the time that the guarantee is requested to the time that the event or change is to take place. Organizational and interpersonal guarantees almost always entail a firm promise for a specific outcome or change by a certain target date.

When you demand a guarantee from someone and that person agrees to it, both of you have disempowered yourselves. First, you as the demander are disempowered by taking something that is supposed to happen in the future as an accomplished fact, when it is anything but that. Second, by focusing on the guarantee, you let go of any responsibility for the outcome, and in so doing, you relinquish your chances of having any impact on the events that are occurring now that could make the outcome happen. Third, your security as implied by the guarantee is now totally in the hands of the guarantor; you have lost control over your own security.

The guarantor is disempowered by promising an outcome or a change that may not be deliverable because he has no awareness of or control over the future. The guarantor is also disempowered by giving you a guarantee without taking it into consideration that his own wants or needs may change over time.

The most obvious example of the problem with guarantees is the high divorce rate that is almost taken for granted today in our society.

Think about it. Two people in their early twenties are told on their wedding day to give each other a firm guarantee that 30 years from today they will feel the same way that they feel right now. Making a guarantee is not the only approach to marriage. Consider the colleague of mine who, when asked if she was getting a divorce after several decades of marriage, replied, "Of course not. I've just decided not to renew my option."

Some frequently heard day-to-day examples of disastrous guarantees are: "Don't worry, the contract is in the bag." "I personally guarantee that Marc will start showing more interest in his work." "I promise to start being nicer to your mother." And of course: "I'll love you forever."

A great deal of disempowerment occurs both in the asking for and in the granting of guarantees, but the most debilitating aspect is that many individuals consciously render themselves inactive until they get a guarantee. A good example of this in business is the often-heard statement, "I won't commit any resources to this project until you guarantee that it will pay off as planned."

Commercial guarantees and warranties are different. They do not promise performance. They promise redress in the event that performance does not occur. This strikes me as a reasonable and realistic statement of a company's or an individual's willingness and commitment to stand behind a product or an action.

The only guarantee that I am ever comfortable giving is a guarantee that I will give my very best effort. My effort is, after all, the only thing that I have total control over. If the event fails, and I honored my guarantee in the process, both parties are in a position to realistically view what went wrong and to learn from it without a great deal of defensiveness. When unrealistic guarantees fail, the result is usually a downward spiral of blame, defensiveness, resentment, and guilt that usually results in a worsening of interpersonal and work relationships.

Incidentally, don't confuse the statement, "I'll give it my best shot," with the statement, "I'll try." *Trying is lying*. It's not that there is any intentional attempt at evasiveness; it's just that when you say you'll try, you're only committing your efforts partway. It's nice to be willing to try, but it also leaves you a way out in case the effort required is more than you initially anticipated. "I'll give it my best shot" says clearly, "Everything I've got, you've got." For me there is also a distinct psychological difference between the two statements. When someone says, "Well, I gave it my best shot," even though the result was a failure, you know the person's self-esteem and self-appreciation are intact. When someone says, "I tried," there's a whine.

A pragmatic approach to dealing with disempowerment by guarantees involves switching the focus away from the future and onto the present. Instead of negotiating specific guarantees that the parties may or may not be able to uphold, you will find much higher payoffs in negotiating current *areas of accountability* that affect future results. Once I am clear about what is expected of me and I have had an opportunity to state my objections, I am in a much better position to fully and realistically commit my effort to the attainment of the goal, and I feel much more secure in being fully answerable for my own actions.

Using Qualifiers

Another block to power is the belief that you must justify your wants or needs. Since you have the absolute right, all the time, to want whatever it is that you want, is not necessary to include the message that it's okay if you don't get all of it.

If you preface clear wants with qualifying phrases, you markedly decrease your chances of obtaining your desired objective and you experience a loss of power in the situation. For example, I certainly don't have to think of a reason to *not* give you what you want when you say to me, "You probably won't want to do this, but . . . ," or, "This might not seem like a very good idea, but . . . ." What you are telling me is that you don't think your request has much value. When you say, "You probably won't agree with this, but . . . ," you set up the probability that you will be exactly right! My all-time favorite qualifier is, "Hey, Hank, you're not going to believe this but . . . ." You're right. If what's coming is not an outright lie, I know that at the least a very heavy exaggeration is on its way, and I've discounted what you're going to say by 50 percent even before you've said it. There are countless qualifying phrases, each one a self-inflicted destroyer of power. All qualifiers give the message that in fact you really don't have the right to get all of what you're asking for. If you don't think you have the right, why should anyone else? After all, who would know better than you?

There's a very simple process that can do wonders for your ability to get more of what you want on a regular basis. It has three steps, and all things being equal, it represents your best shot.

1. Get the other person's attention.
2. Make the demand or request as briefly and as concisely as possible.
3. Say absolutely nothing else!

Take Carl, who wants tomorrow off and must get Perry's okay to get it.

C: Perry, got a minute?
P: What is it?
C: I'd like tomorrow off.

STOP! The next person to speak loses control of the process.

This is Carl's best chance of getting the day off. If Perry wants or needs more information, it's up to him to ask for it. If, let's say, a whole day off isn't available but a half day is, Carl is in a much better position in "forcing" Perry to qualify the request than he would be if he had qualified it himself with, say, "I'd like all of tomorrow off, but if you can't let me have it, the morning would do."

By staying silent after you make your request, you put the granter into the position of having to justify why the request shouldn't be granted instead of assuming that you have to justify why it should be. If you remain silent, almost anything that the granter says will be in service to your getting the request granted. You are in the best position even if the initial response is no. First, once the no is delivered, you are in a position to ask, "What's your objection?" If after the objection is explained the answer to your request is still no, it simply means that what you requested isn't available, and sooner you are aware of this, the better for all concerned.

On the front end of the strategy, *anything* that Carl puts between getting Perry's attention and making the request is going to markedly decrease Carl's chances of getting what he wants. Compare the interaction above with this more typical one:

C: Perry.
P: What is it?
C: I know that we are running a little behind and that time is a
     little tight right now, but you don't suppose that I could take
     tomorrow off anyway, do you?

CHAPTER 4

Power Regained

Although many people experience disempowerment as a chronic condition, they do not have to continue to experience it in this way. Since actualizing your power is purely a function of what's going on right here, right now, there are steps that you can take immediately to reverse the condition or to continue to build on your existing power base.

Chapter 3 surfaced and discussed many of the more damaging methods of self-disempowerment. If any or all of these are relevant, you first and most obvious step toward regaining lost power is to address each one directly. Although the techniques presented here may at first require a little intestinal fortitude, they do not involve great personal risk and are relatively simple to pull off.

Overestimating Yourself

When you begin a program aimed at regaining or increasing your power, you may find it difficult to accurately estimate both your ability and the ensuing risks of failure or rejection. When you lack sufficient data to judge whether or not you have the ability to get what you want, you are likely to underestimate, rather than overestimate, your power. This condition is the result of years of fear of failure, societal "shoulds," and dealing with such platitudes as "Be humble" and "Always put others first." *When in doubt*, I recommend that you overestimate your power.

By overestimating your power, you are probably either still underestimating it a little or hitting it right on the nose. And if, in fact, you do overestimate your power, it won't be by much, and usually the most that you risk is a slap on the wrist, some embarrassment, or someone temporarily being upset with you. All a bit painful, I grant you, but none of it lethal.

When you overestimate your power and effectiveness, the environment lets you know pretty quickly that you have done so—or that you were correct—and you can learn from the experience and modify your behavior accordingly the next time. On the other hand, when you underestimate your power and effectiveness, you never have a way of knowing this. Therefore, your tendency will be to keep carefully and safely polishing your current behaviors over and over. By underestimating your power, you give up the opportunity to test your current boundaries for strength and effectiveness.

An enjoyable variation of this approach is called "Let's Pretend." Here you play at being powerful so that you can test it for "fit" and comfort. First sit down with pencil and paper and brainstorm a list of things that symbolize "powerful" to *you*. For example, what types of clothes, accessories, books, colors, brands, music, decor, and so forth, suggests "powerful"? Second, choose from the list the things that are at least marginally comfortable for you and then try them! A word of caution: At this stage, don't make yourself particularly conspicuous or vulnerable. The purpose here is for you to provide your self with a safe, enjoyable way of testing some new perspectives. Years back, one of the things I did was to wear my cowboy hat when I watched *Maverick*.

The next time you're invited to a theme party or a masquerade, or the next time that Halloween rolls around, try going as Attila the Hun instead of as the Easter bunny and see if it isn't just a little more enjoyable and exciting.

Obtaining Closure

An axiom that lies at the core of all personal and organizational effectiveness is: Good endings make for good beginnings. Many people reduce their effectiveness and lessen their power by carrying around huge amounts of unfinished business day in and day out. One of the first and most important steps toward increasing your power is to be able, fully and wholly, to say goodbye to things that are finished.

You have a large, but nevertheless finite, amount of energy. Any energy that you expend in regretting lost opportunities, seething over past injustices, or suffering over long-gone relationships is energy that is not available to you to invest in current goals and relationships. In other words, not until you say goodbye to things that are over can you fully say hello to the next opportunity or relationship that emerges on the scene. In extreme cases, being locked into the past can eventually cause a chronic downward spiral, since current opportunities are lost again and again because time and energy are being wasted in agonizing over past lost opportunities. The more opportunities you lose, the more you have to regret, and the more opportunities you lose—and you are caught in a vicious cycle.

One way to get closure is to mourn—rather than to seethe, regret, suffer, or ignore—loss. *Mourning* is the act of saying goodbye to things or relationships that are gone and will never return again. On the societal scale, most cultures prescribe long and complex mourning rituals in order to allow the individuals involved to honor and experience the loss fully and then go on with their lives. Although mourning over someone's death is accepted, unfortunately mourning is rarely seen as appropriate in any other context.

A simple approach to regaining your power is to allow yourself to feel as bad as you really feel about something that is gone for as long as it takes you to get over it. The sooner that the mourning is finished, the sooner your full energy will be available to you to pursue your current needs and goals. For example, being passed over for a promotion that I had thought I honestly deserved is ample cause for me to feel bad. By giving myself permission to feel as bad as I feel until I no longer feel this way, I will be over the experience sooner and be in a position to pursue the next promotion or option that comes up. If I choose, on the other hand, to slough the whole thing off as unimportant, I risk having to deal with the sadness and resentment indefinitely. You can't kill your feelings; you can just bury them *alive*. Please note that I am not advocating that you tearfully make the rounds of everyone you know to tell each one how you're suffering! The mourning process can be worked through alone or, better, with someone who is close to you and is genuinely concerned for your welfare.

Another advantage of being willing to honestly mourn permanent losses is that you learn to distinguish those losses that deserve the mourning from those losses that do not. That is, by *not* mourning major losses that deserve it, you risk letting every tiny perceived rejection and minor loss have the same draining effect on you as the more important ones.

A second technique for getting closure is to actually do the things that it would take to finish up the unfinished business. How often have you found yourself saying, "Boy, I wish I'd said . . . ," or "What I should have told that jerk was . . . !" Until you actually say the words you are probably condemning yourself to months, if not years, of reliving the experience and rewriting the ending. If it is possible to actually confront the individual and do whatever you have to do to get closure, this is the best approach. So tell a good neighbor that you resent his not returning your power drill, or tell your aging parents that you love them. In many cases, however, it is either impossible or inadvisable to confront the other individual directly, as with the bully way back in high school who made 8:00 a.m. to 3:30 p.m. a nightmare for you, or your new boss, who just recently unjustly called you to task. When this is the case, a simple and effective way to get closure is to use the open-chair technique.

1. Place two straight-backed chairs about 6 feet from each other.
2. Sit in one of the chairs and imagine that the person with whom you have the unfinished business is sitting in the other chair.
3. Get a good image of what the person looked like at your last meeting.
4. State, as fully as you can, what you want the other person to hear from you.
5. Then get up and switch chairs and, playing the part of the person who has just heard what you had to say, respond to "you" in the chair just vacated.
6. Continue the dialogue by reversing roles and switching chairs as each new point is made until you are finished.

Although this may seem a little awkward at first, this technique actually allows you to achieve closure by doing what you need to do. Since you are doing this alone, allow yourself to express yourself as fully as you possibly can. If the issue is one of anger, really shout; if it's one of being rejected, really let the other person know what it feels like. The fact that the other person isn't physically there is really of little importance.

While I'm on the subject, this technique is also excellent for resolving issues of internal approach–approach conflict, for example, "I want to go home for the Christmas holidays/I want to stay here for the Christmas holidays." Here you play the two competing sides of yourself in the two chairs. The more polarized your views are in the beginning, the higher the probability that you will surface most, if not all, of the pros and cons of both positions. Make your opening arguments as strong as you can from both positions: "We [the two competing sides of you] haven't seen Mom in six months and she really misses us." This might be countered with, "Are you aware of that really great Christmas Eve party that we are invited to, that we will miss if we go home?" If you reach a deadlock in either or both positions, see if you can make a deal with the "other" side, for example, "I'm willing to go home, but only for two days. What do you think?"

A third technique for getting closure involves choosing to finish what you are doing before tackling the new problem or issue. However, conditions often demand that you stop working on one problem in order to deal with a more pressing one. When this occurs, take the time to *bracket* the unfinished piece. This entails acknowledging that the piece is unfinished and perhaps even making a note of it, so that you can get back to it to complete it as soon as the crisis is over.

Making Clearer Decisions

Essential to the expression of power is making clearer decisions. Since all power resides in conscious choice, it follows that *how* that choice is made is going to be a key determining factor in how powerful you are. The first thing to recognize is that all decisions are subjective. The moment that you say, "I want," or "I choose," you are totally in the realm of subjectivity. The statement "I want productivity up in this unit by 4 percent by the end of this quarter" is just as subjective as the statement "I want to go to Hawaii for my vacation this year" or "I'll take the red convertible."

Since all decisions are subjective, all decisions are, by definition, based on *values*. Being clear about what is important to you, and accepting of this, is the first step toward making better, more satisfying decisions. This rarely means that holding one value necessarily means excluding another, but it does mean that you will need to establish clear priorities. For example, given that each is valuable, which takes precedence, quality or profitability, efficiency or effectiveness, authentic relationships or warm, supportive relationships, the organization or the individuals, being fair or being right? It doesn't matter which you choose, all things being equal; it matters only that you be clear and comfortable with your value choices. Since in reality all things are rarely equal, being clear about your values will save you the time and confusion of struggling to get clear on your values at the same time as you are struggling to come up with a solid decision based on these values.

Once you are clear about your values, the next step is to be clear and comfortable with the process that you use to make a decision. For me, decision making is a six-step process. When I screw something up, and I assure you that I do, it's usually because I have gone off, half-cocked, and started with Step 5 instead of with Step 1.

Step 1. Get Clear on the Objective of Your Decision

Before you put any work or time into making a decision, you need to be clear about the decision's objective. That is, what will a good decision look like when you get one? It doesn't matter whether you are working alone or with a group, nor does it matter what particular decision-making mechanism you intend to use—ranking, forced choice, paired comparisons, and so forth. Unless this first step is accomplished, the whole decision-making process will represent little more than a crapshoot. Actually, the more time you spend on this first step, the easier the balance of the process will be and the less time you will need for it. Suppose that you and a friend are planning to go on vacation together. You need to begin by getting clear about whether you are looking for relaxation or diversion, places that are new and unknown or places that are comfortable and familiar, and so on. Hopefully, you can see that getting clarity on your respective needs and values will make the process of deciding a lot easier and more workable and will also increase the probability that you will have a good time together on the vacation.

For example, if your idea of a great vacation is a two-week junket to the casinos in Las Vegas and your friend's dream vacation is a two-week walking tour of the bird sanctuaries of North Carolina, you have some real problems ahead of you if you don't address this issue first. Let's say that you jointly opt for inexpensive foreign travel, as it seems to be the best choice to give both of you most of what you want. Keep in mind that the prime agreement is that you both want to take this vacation together. This first step sets the stage and is the controlling factor for the entire decision-making process.

Step 2. Gather Data

Whereas the act of deciding is a purely subjective process, gathering and analyzing the information you need to make the best decision are purely *objective*. Step 1, clarity on the objective of the decision, tells you what you need to know. Most of the information that you need to make high-quality decisions is like money in the street. It's just lying there, waiting to be picked up. What you need to know is determined by Step 1. Getting the information is Step 2. I'm sure that you are aware that when you accept assumptions when real data are available, you deserve what happens to you. "It seemed like a good idea at the time" is rarely looked upon compassionately today.

A problem that is almost as great as not having enough information is having too much information. When objectivity is deified, the article of faith is that more information is always better than less information. This produces such statements as "Let's table it for further study," "Let's do another attitude survey," and "Let's hire a consultant." You have all this information coming in from who knows where, in service to who knows what, and while you are feverishly trying to make sense out of all of it, the boat has left! The timeliness of a decision is often as important as the information that contributes to making it. Although I don't necessarily advocate this for anyone but myself, I want to be just objective enough to let new information in and not one bit more objective than that. Step 1 tells you not only what information you need but also how much information you need.

Staying with the vacation illustration, once you're clear about what will constitute a good vacation in terms of your current wants, you can start to collect relevant information about what is available—brochures, information from travel agencies, and so forth.

Step 3. Clarify the Unknown

Step 3 is the easiest to overlook because it is the least obvious. Now that you're clear about what is important (Step 1) and you have all the information that is available (Step 2), you need to be clear about what you still need to know but *don't*. Thus you don't know what the weather will actually be like, how crowded the areas might be, or what else may be available that isn't advertised in the brochures.

Step 4. Make Assumptions

As mentioned earlier, if you opt for assumptions when data are available, you generally deserve whatever happens to you. But that statement was made in reference to Step 2. In Step 4 assumptions are essential. When you are clear about what is unknown, Step 3, you are ready to make assumptions to cover the blank area.

When data are unavailable, you are a lot better off making clear assumptions, even if they turn out to be totally wrong, than you are by remaining unaware or unconcerned about potentially relevant considerations. Even if the assumptions do turn out to be incorrect, you can learn from the process. As an example, had the industrial planners of the first half of this century taken the time to make assumptions about the unknown, we probably wouldn't be facing the pollution nightmare of the second half.

Every once in a great while, you'll sit down and work out all the assumptions and they'll be exactly right, just as if you had had the relevant data. Just as rarely, you'll sit down and make all the wrong assumptions. Ninety-eight times out of a hundred you are going to end up somewhere in between these two extremes, which puts you in a better position than if you had not responded at all. The assumptions that you make cover the blank area, that is, the unknown information that might be relevant.

Step 5. Generate Alternatives

When you are clear that Steps 2, 3, and 4 are covering Step 1, you are in a position to generate alternatives, always going for a minimum of three. For example, "We could go to southern Europe, to Mexico, or to Upper Volta"—each of which would fill the bill.

Step 6. Make a Conscious Choice Among the Alternatives

I've covered the nature and function of conscious choice and its relationship to power pretty thoroughly. The only thing that I'd like to underscore is that the clearer the criteria you develop in Step 1, the easier and more potent will be your actual decision.

Getting Clear Expectations

A complaint of middle and lower management that I hear frequently is, "My boss won't tell me what is expected of me." There is no question that to the extent that this condition exists between levels of management, there will be missed deadlines, marginal productivity, strained interpersonal relationships, disappointment on the part of the superior manager, and sometimes traumatic insecurity on the part of the lower-level manager. The question is: What do you do about it?

The first and most frequently used approach to this problem is to complain about the condition to whoever is willing to listen. Although this alternative will do little to increase your personal and organizational effectiveness, it is not as bad as it may seem. First, it shows that your heart is in the right place; that is, you'd be happy to do your job if only somebody would take the time to tell you what it is. Second, you have adequately protected your rear—you can always say, "But nobody told me that I had to do that." Third, you now have the time to concentrate on important matters, such as getting along well with others, making the right connections, and developing your crossword puzzle skills. Since you are accountable for nothing, you have to produce nothing!

The second approach is to confront your boss about what is expected of you. Although this approach is much more results-oriented, it does involve some risks. First, you must be very careful to get the expectations in *specific terms.* If you fail to do this, you still don't know what's expected of you and you are right back where you started, only the next time the matter comes up, you risk the boss's puzzlement and displeasure about why you don't know your own job. Also, unless you get it exactly right the first time, you risk continuously having to ask, "What do you want me to do now?"

A third option is to clarify your expectations first and then confront your boss as to what he'd like. Before you see your boss, sit down and design your job or role exactly the way that you would like it to be. This entails being very clear about the areas of responsibility that you want and that you don't want. It's also important to cast your job or role in terms of *results,* since it's a lot easier to get the desired authority if you can show how it will affect productivity or work relationships. This option is quite effective and has the least risk associated with it.

There is a fourth option, and although it carries the most risk, it is also the one that carries the greatest potential for increasing your power and effectiveness. There is a precondition here of a solid, supportive working relationship between you and your boss. The first step is to be absolutely clear about how you want your job or duties designed. The second step is to simply ask your boss for a list of all the things that you do *not* have the authority to do. If it's possible, get the list in writing and have it initialed. From this point on, anything that is not expressed explicitly on that list is within your scope of authority. One of the more salient tenets of effective management is that all authority that is not expressly and specifically claimed by upper management is automatically at the discretion of lower management. What many subordinate managers fail to see is that the responsibility for putting this tenet to work is in *their* hands.

Even if your boss is hesistant to give you such a list, you are in an excellent position to start negotiating the relevant areas of your job responsibility. Along with this, the boss will be in a somewhat defensive position of having to "show cause" why authority is not available, rather than being in the traditional role of granting requests.

If the working relationship is not supportive enough for you to initiate or negotiate this approach overtly, the next best step is for you to initiate it covertly. In each situation in which you are not sure whether or not you have the authority to act, you must first assess the attending risk in the situation. If the risk is not worth taking, check the situation out with your boss first. If, on the other hand, the risk is reasonable, and most of the time it will be, assume that you have the authority to do what you want. If you assume the authority and succeed, you will have set a precedent and will, in all probability, increase not only your authority in that area but your power as well. Even if you assume the authority and fail, you will still have taken the lesser risk in my opinion. That is, it is better to risk failure by making a mistake than to risk failure by doing nothing.

A few years back, when Eric was about 10, he was invited to spend New Year's Eve at his friend Robbie's house while my wife and I went to a party. The kids were given the proverbial list of do's and don'ts and then left in the care of Robbie's sister. The next morning, Robbie's mother, upon looking out the upstairs bathroom window, noticed two sets of small footprints in the newly fallen snow on the lower roof of the den. With clearcut evidence and proof positive, she bellowed for the kids to come up to the bathroom. Confronting them with the evidence, she demanded, "Who told you two that you could climb out on the roof?" They replied quietly but confidently, "Nobody, but nobody said that we couldn't either." Guess who won that one!

An old axiom of power that is well worth remembering is: It is always easier to get forgiveness after than it is to get permission before.

Getting Centered

Powerlessness is most often expressed in physical ways. Some more common indicators are shortness of breath, "butterflies" in the stomach, shaky voice, and trembling, all of which may sometimes be accompanied by visceral constriction. The common interpretation is, "I am powerless; therefore, I feel this way." The *reality* is, "I feel this way; therefore, I am powerless."

The essence of power is self-support, not only psychological but physical as well. When you allow yourself to become distracted by worry, anxiety, or the threat of some external stimulus, you tend to forget to breathe. The result of this is reflexive, shallow breathing, which introduces less oxygen into the bloodstream. It's the absence of oxygen that results in the "butterflies," lightheadedness, and other physical symptoms of powerlessness.

To express power effectively, you must be able to use all the channels of communication that are available to you. Your body posture, tone of voice, and eye contact must be consistent with the message that you are conveying and must support the clarity of the message as well. The term *getting centered* refers to taking the time to get in touch with what you are feeling so that the feeling component of the message is consistent with the content. The term also refers to the condition of using yourself as your prime means of support. Even if three out of four messages that you are sending simultaneously to the other person indicate power, you'll probably not be seen as being powerful because of the fourth, countermanding message. For example, it is very difficult, if not impossible, to express yourself powerfully if you are slouched down in a chair with your chin tucked into your chest.

The next time you find yourself suffering from a severe case of powerlessness—when the boss yells, "Get in here!" or you are about to explain to the board why the project failed, or you got caught walking on the roof, or you are in any situation that has given you "stage fright"—try the following procedure:

1. *Attend to your breathing.* Breathe deeply and slowly, so that your stomach moves out and in with each complete respiration. Breathe in through your nose and breathe out through your mouth, as if you were a pump. Breathe easily and naturally, and avoid hyperventilating.

2. *Attend to your posture.* Use your backbone to support your body. If you are seated, use the chairback only to help you maintain a comfortable balance. Plant your feet firmly on the floor, about 12 to 14 inches apart. Feel the floor entirely with each foot. Fold your arms comfortably or extend them on the chair's armrests. *Relax!*

3. *Attend to the here-and-now.* Instead of wondering or worrying about what is going to happen next, focus your attention on what is going on right now. Silently, see how many things in the immediate environment you are aware of. Think these out in complete sentences: "I'm aware of the blue pencil on the desk," "I'm aware of the sound of a truck going by," "I'm aware of the gray cloud in the oil painting on the far wall," and so on. Stay with this process until the time for the "event."

Give it a try; it really works! Remember that all stage fright, or anxiety, is a direct function of being a few moments into the future. Doing whatever you can to maintain your awareness of the present and to use yourself for support will go a long way toward reducing your sense of vulnerability and increasing your power when the moment of engagement actually occurs.

Using Powerful Words

In my opinion, one of the greatest apologies of all time came from the pen of T. S. Eliot when his character Sweeney, a symbolic figure who appears in several of his poems, explained, "I've got to use words when I talk to you." Although it often is the only means of conveying the content of a message, the spoken or written word is frequently also the least effective in conveying impact. The impact of a message is usually imparted through nonverbal communication channels, such as tone of voice, gestures, facial expressions, and body posture. For instance, simply telling a child that you love her is much less powerful than smiling and hugging her as you say the words to her softly. The more nonverbal messages you use to back up your message, the higher the probability that your message will be received clearly by the other person. This is an essential first step in getting what you want and it is the essence of contact.

The fact that clear nonverbal communication is very important does not mean that your choice of words is unimportant. Even when your content is clear and your nonverbal communications are supportive, you may soften or subvert your message by using *powerless* words. Here are a few tips that may help you to express yourself more powerfully.

Avoid Euphemisms

The use of euphemisms is an intentional attempt to soften contact. The underlying assumption is that if I couch what I want to say in softer terms, you will be more ready to accept what I have to say. It's much like sugarcoating a pill to get a child to swallow it. I suppose that there is some validity in doing this. The problem is that at the same time as I succeed in getting you to lessen your resistance to what I am saying, the impact of my words is lessened also.

Here are some euphemisms in current use: Organizational scapegoating is now called "producing creative tension"; organizational tyranny is known as "dynamic leadership"; taking unfair advantage is referred to as "driving a hard bargain"; taxation is now called "revenue enhancement." Try this for comparison: "My father has gone to his reward" as opposed to "My father is dead."

There are two problems with euphemisms. When you *speak* in euphemisms, your impact on other people tends to be softened. When you *think* in euphemisms, you tend to avoid taking full responsibility for your actions or your views, thereby softening the impact on yourself. A military report might say "pre-emptive retaliation" when it means attack first, but isn't that a nice way of phrasing it?

Avoid Qualifying Words

I mentioned earlier that qualifying statements will have a highly negative effect on your ability to get what you want. Inappropriate use of qualifying words can have an equally negative effect. Used appropriately, such words as *just, only,* and *little* are as effective as any. But when these words (and others like them) are needlessly dropped into the middle of a statement, they can undermine the entire intent of the message.

Take the statement "I just wanted to say that I liked your little presentation" and the statement "I want you to know that I really liked your presentation." The second statement is much more powerful than the first. To begin with, if you use the word *just,* you imply that the compliment is in itself relatively unimportant; and the word *little* belittles the presentation. Also, by placing the word *just* where it is, you tend to cast the statement into the past tense. The unavoidable implication of this is that the compliment was an afterthought. More important, use of the word *just* strongly implies that you are apologizing for giving the compliment—"It's *only little* me who is saying this." Use of qualifying words not only disempowers you, it also robs the other person of experiencing the full impact of your message.

Eschew Obfuscation

I'm a lover of paradox, and this subheading is my all-time favorite wall poster. It, of course, translates as: Avoid expressing yourself in terms that are confusing to other people. Forms of verbal expression such as professional jargon, argot, and street slang are quite appropriate and effective when you are conversing with someone who shares your cultural or professional background. When this is not the case, the use of jargon is not appropriate.

When you intentionally use jargon with people outside the appropriate setting, you may be attempting to impress those people with your expertise in order to have a greater impact on them, or you may be attempting to impress them with your special membership in some group. More often than not, instead of being impressed, people will be confused, tuned out, and turned off by you. As a matter of fact, I take a rather extreme view on this point. If I am unclear about what you are saying and you are the expert, then you must be totally confused! I realize that this is not the only possible explanation for my not understanding your words, but it is the one that I will usually choose.

Use Expletives Carefully and Creatively

The word *expletive* refers to what most of us commonly think of as curse words, swear words, or just plain "talking dirty." In the area of expletives, concern for what is tasteful and acceptable and for what is not is critical. The obvious rule of thumb is: When in doubt, *don't*! However, if the particular expletive is within your boundary for good taste and is not likely to violate the sensibilities of others, what the hell, go ahead and use it! The very fact that the use of expletives is such a touchy subject for so many people indicates the power of expletives and their ability to have an impact. For example, how memorable would the following statements have been if the expletives had been deleted to read as follows?

"Darn the torpedoes, full speed ahead!"
"War is heck!"
"I'm mad as all get out, and I'm not going to take it anymore!"

Some years back, when Eric was about 8 years old, I took him trolling for bluefish. As luck would have it, he hooked a big one and fought it as long as he could. I took over for a while but handed the rod back to him as I brought the fish in alongside the boat, since I wanted him to land it. As I handed him the rod, the tip dropped a little and the blue spit the lure and took off. Eric's immediate and *reflexive* response was to scream, "#$@ &ing fish!" I consider that *highly* inappropriate behavior for an 8-year-old, and Eric knew I felt that way. In fact, not only had he lost the fish, but the instant after he let go with the expletive, his face clearly showed his terror that those were the last two words he would utter in this life. I sized up the situation and responded the only way I could: "Son, sometimes there just isn't any other way to say it."

Using Statements

In normal communication with others, there are two basic grammatical forms for dealing with information: statements, which are used for imparting information, and questions, which are used for eliciting information. Although the purpose of questions is to get the information that is needed, all too often questions are used inappropriately to soften contact or to gain support from another person. In these cases, a clear, declarative statement would be much more effective. Three specific cases in which the use of questions causes disempowerment warrant mention.

The first case can be subsumed under this golden rule: Never ask a question if you do not want an answer! In the nonwork environment there seems to be a little less violation of this than in the work setting. For example, very few parents ask their kids if they think it would be a good idea to do their homework, go to bed, or finish their vegetables. They can pretty much count on how their kids will respond.

In the work setting the violations seem to abound. Often, in an attempt to be democratic, a superior will ask subordinates for their opinions when the situation clearly does not warrant any further discussion, or when the superior clearly knows already what the desired outcome is going to be. Once you ask such a question, you, as the superior, are stuck. You must deal with and honor all opinions given regardless of how long it takes. And as a result, there will always be some members of the group who will be frustrated because they will realize that their views never really had a chance for consideration in the first place. Also, when you choose to do this, you put yourself into the untenable and unnecessary position of trying to convince subordinates that their suggestions and recommendations are not quite appropriate. Thus you are not listening to what they are saying to get more information; instead, you are listening to their input so that you can formulate arguments against it. If you attempt this tactic too often, you will eventually be seen as a con artist, rather than as an enlightened, participative leader.

The second case against the inappropriate use of questions occurs when you want to get a confirming opinion from someone with expertise. Suppose that you have a clear opinion about something and you'd like to use me as a sounding board to get another view. You ask me my opinion on this subject, and my response totally agrees with your privately held opinion. Who feels good when this happens? You do. Who is the hero? I am, since I am the one who confirmed your opinion. Suppose, on the other hand, you ask me my opinion on the subject and my response totally opposes your privately held opinion. Now how important is your opinion to you?

Although there is nothing wrong in getting other people's opinions, you are always more effective when you state your opinion first. When you do this and then elicit another opinion, you are affirming your position yourself instead of asking someone else to do it for you. Then, if you do get the corroboration, it's doubly supportive. If you do not get it, your opinion is still every bit as valid as the opposing view.

The third case of disempowerment through inappropriate questions is the most pervasive, the least obvious, and the most self-destructive. This form occurs when you hide a statement in a question. The hidden statement often starts with "Wouldn't you agree that . . .?" "Don't you think . . .?" or "Isn't it so that . . .?" Whenever you hide a statement in a question, three things occur that set the stage for disempowerment.

First, when you ask a question like this, you automatically put yourself in a one-down position. Suppose that I respond, "Good grief, no! I never think that!" Now how powerful are you? And if I do agree with you, you get the agreement and I get the credit, since you set me up as the empowering agent.

Second, when you ask a question when you are really making a statement, there is a high risk that I will become confused, since what sounds like a legitimate question really isn't. You ask, "Don't you think that . . .?" I say, "No." Then you say, "Yes, but don't you think that . . .?" and I reply, "*No*, it's . . ." Then you come back with, "*Yes, but* don't you think . . .?" and my reply is "*No, dammit*, it's . . .!!!" By the second "Yes, but . . .," I have written you off as not dealing with a full deck, since I have told you my position three times and you still haven't heard me. At this point, I will be totally confused and frustrated, and you will have severely disempowered yourself because you were unable to get what you wanted, which was to *tell* me something.

Third, when you hide a statement in a question, it has an undesired effect on the listener. The usual intent of this tactic is to soften the resistance by cajoling the other person into agreement. Frequently it has just the opposite effect. With me, when someone begins a statement with "Wouldn't you agree that . . . ," I immediately start to withdraw because I am getting a faint but clear message that I am being set up. I am being asked to agree with something before I have even heard what it is. My tendency is to have a "no" ready simply as an act of self-protection.

In sum, questions are effective when you want information or when you honestly want other people's involvement, support, or participation. In all other cases, a clear statement of your position, desires, or views has the highest probability of getting you what you want. In fact, you are even better off if you preface your real questions with a clear statement such as "I am confused about paragraph two on this page. Will you please explain . . . ?" In this way, you tell the other person what your concern or current awareness is, which helps that person to respond more accurately to your needs.

Saying No

Of all the ways that people go about disempowering themselves, none is more obvious than being unwilling to say no when that is the appropriate response. The tendency to say yes or to agree by remaining silent, when open disagreement is appropriate, results in four separate conditions of disempowerment. Two of these affect you and two affect the other individual.

First, every time you mean no and say yes or withhold your objection, you end up doing things that you do not want to do. It doesn't matter whether it's getting stuck with 3 hours of overtime when you wanted to go home or with 30 years of marriage because you said "I do" when you really "didn't." Each time you say yes when you mean no, or go along with something against your own wants or better judgment, it is *you* who are making a victim out of you, not the other person!

Second, when you withhold your objection by remaining silent, you still end up taking full responsibility for the outcome, the same as the people who clearly and loudly agreed. You will find yourself in the somewhat awkward position of being recognized for being effective in supporting an outcome that you did not want to occur. And if the event doesn't work out, no one will be very sympathetic to your plea, "Well, I really didn't think it was a very good idea at the time." I can't speak for anyone else, but I know for myself that the pain I feel when I make a strong case for something I believe in and end up being proven wrong is much less than the pain I feel when, having said absolutely nothing, I end up being proven right. If I ever get around to having a family crest made, the motto emblazoned over the shield will read (in Latin), "Sometimes Wrong But Rarely in Doubt."

The third condition relates to the person that you are refusing to say no to. Every time you withhold your honest objection, you rob that person in two ways. First, you deny her your unique viewpoint. Your viewpoint represents a new alternative for the other person to consider. When that alternative is not brought into play, the result is a potential loss of power. Second, you rob her of the right to say no right back to you. Suppose I'm engaged in an activity that appears to me to be going rather well. From your view, it appears that I am heading for failure, but since you don't want to be seen as being disruptive or negative, you say nothing. Let me assure you that if it turns out later that your view was the correct one, I will not thank you for your willing compliance or your polite silence. In the work setting, many good ideas are lost and mediocre results attained simply because of a subordinate's failure to understand the difference between expressing disagreement with the boss's viewpoint and refusing the boss's lawful direction. In the vast majority of cases, the first is highly valued while the second is not.

The fourth condition can easily be illustrated by the statement "If I can't trust you to say no to me when you think or feel no, then I can't trust your yesses either. Therefore, you will never be fully available as a resource to me."

Some years back, I was doing some training work with a colleague and close friend from Montreal. Just prior to his coming down to work with me, another opportunity arose for us to work together on the same trip, and I accepted. Fully anticipating a happy, positive response, as was his usual style, I called to tell him the good news. His response to this golden opportunity for more work with me was a quiet but firm no. He mumbled something about "family," but being in a mixed state of rage and shock, I barely heard him. Not only had he said no, he had said it to *me*. (Two records broken in a single day.) After we said goodbye, the rage began to subside, and in its place, panic began to emerge. I had rather foolishly accepted the second contract without first checking it out with him. Now I was stuck! After an hour or so of hand wringing and deep sweats, I remembered another colleague in Boston who would be very effective in the position. I gave her a call, and she accepted the contract on the spot.

My good friend from Montreal did me three big favors in saying no to me. First, he withheld what would have been a marginal resource. He clearly didn't want to work this time, and had he accepted, for whatever reason, I would have been stuck with his halfhearted support. Also, by withholding his grudging support, he forced me into the position of having to find the solid support that I did want and, in this case, badly needed. The third favor, and probably the best, was that he established a much more solid working relationship with me. I know now that when he gives me a yes, it is a clear, unqualified yes, and that I can then count on the very best that he has to offer.

I believe that there are two main reasons why so many people have difficulty saying no. First, they believe that saying no will be harmful to the other person. Second, they believe that saying no will damage the relationship with the person that they are saying it to.

There are two techniques that can be used to lessen these perceived negative side effects. First, keep in mind that when you choose to say no to someone, that no is for right now, not forever. A statement such as "I'm not available at this time, but please get back to me again if you think that I can be of some help later on" goes a long way toward reducing needless guilt and establishing or maintaining a positive relationship.

Second, keep in mind that you always have three choices in responding to a request or a demand from someone else: (1) "Yes, I will", (2) "No, I won't", (3) "Yes, I will under the following circumstances. . . ." You may have a tendency to forget, or to fear making, the third choice, with the result that if you say yes, you consciously victimize yourself, and if you say no, you may be letting a friend or colleague down when you don't want to. The third option allows you to give *wholehearted partial* support—for example, "I don't have twenty dollars available, but I can lend you ten"—which frequently will be warmly and gratefully received.

CHAPTER 5

Resistance

In today's modern organizations there has been a growing emphasis on the need for collaboration, cooperation, and trust. This trend has resulted in management development programs designed specifically to get managers to work together as teams, and to share, rather than compete for, resources, and to focus on productivity rather than on politics, in order to attain individual and organizational objectives. There is no question that this approach is productive and essential for organizational growth and human development, particularly in light of today's economic and technological conditions.

However, the problem that seems to arise from this overall emphasis on trust, cooperation, and sharing is that there is a strong tendency to discount and view negatively other behaviors, such as competition, anger, and resistance. But as discussed earlier, these behaviors are not necessarily negative, nor are the others necessarily positive. Each human capacity has the potential to produce an appropriate and effective outcome under the proper circumstances. To discount *any* aspect of human interaction is to limit your resources and to reduce the range of choices that are available to you, which in turn results in your disempowerment and in the loss of effectiveness in the organization.

A human behavior that frequently comes under fire is *resistance*. If cooperation is seen as universally positive, its opposite, resistance, is usually seen as negative. How many times have you heard the admonition: "Don't be defensive!" There is even a personal growth model, the marathon lab, that is specifically designed to assist participants in overcoming or breaking through their defenses. In my view, there is a time to cooperate and a time to resist. One of the most difficult tasks for managers and for trainers in the field of human resources develement is to know when resistance is appropriate and how to express it appropriately, so that the results are positive for all concerned.

Some definitions are needed before we get into the positive aspects of resistance.

Power and Resistance

Just as power is the ability to get what you want from the environment, given what is available, *resistance* is the ability to avoid getting what you don't want from the environment. Power is a means to an end, not an end in itself, and it is solely a function of the individual. Resistance is an expression of power, in that not getting what you don't want is every bit as important and beneficial to you as is getting what you do want.

The relationship between power and resistance can be seen in Figure 9. Getting what you want and avoiding what you do not want are both positive conditions. The two negative conditions can be seen

Figure 9. Power/resistance model.

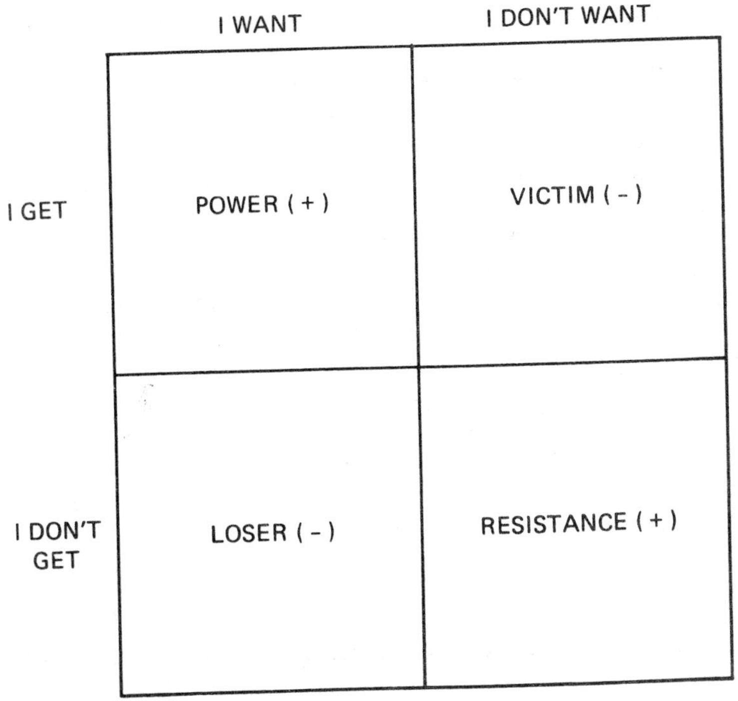

	I WANT	I DON'T WANT
I GET	POWER (+)	VICTIM (-)
I DON'T GET	LOSER (-)	RESISTANCE (+)

as (1) being a loser, that is, wanting something but not getting it, and (2) being a victim, that is, ending up with things that you clearly want no part of. The obvious strategy is to expand the positive areas and diminish the negative ones. Although most people can see power as I have defined it as a positive thing, it seems to be much more difficult for them to view resistance positively; in fact, it is often mistakenly viewed as being out and out negative. This negative view is manifested in such statements as "You're not being cooperative," "You should learn to compromise," and "You've got to go along to get along." These statements are appropriate under certain conditions, but they are extremely disempowering when swallowed whole as "shoulds" or as the right way to be. The higher your ability to resist when resistance is appropriate, the less likely you are to end up as a victim.

Think about the last time you made a New Year's resolution. As a young adult, I made New Year's resolutions every year, many of them the same year after year. As time went on, I stopped making them. If this happened to you too, how come, like me, you used to make resolutions but don't anymore? Chances are that your answer will be the same as mine: I didn't keep them. The next question is: Why do people tend not to keep New Year's resolutions or any other promises they make to themselves?

The Topdog–Underdog Continuum

As discussed in Chapter 2, one way to view the human personality is in terms of polarities. That is, all human characteristics and capacities are to be looked at in terms of opposites, that is, love–hate, strong–weak, introvert–extrovert, dominant–submissive, and so on. One of the more salient of these dimensions is topdog–underdog (see Figure 10). This is what prevents most people from sticking to their resolutions.

Figure 10.   Topdog/underdog continuum.

Topdog

Underdog

The topdog is that part of you that houses your drive, ambition, endurance, and self-improvement needs, for example, the need to lose 20 pounds, strive toward getting the degree, quit smoking. The underdog is that part of you that consistently and irrevocably screws up all the topdog's plans, dreams, and objectives. Say you make a commitment to lose 20 pounds, but you make that commitment two weeks before Christmas. Or you promise yourself that you are going to control your temper, but then you accept a luncheon invitation from the one individual who can set you screaming within ten minutes. You make the promise to yourself with the best of intentions, but somehow it always gets fouled up. The usual response to the failure is a quick shot of guilt and self-contempt and a firmer resolve to lick the problem *this* time. And so it goes, until eventually the white flag goes up, accompanied by a disgruntled sigh of "Oh, the hell with it." After you break a promise or a resolution to yourself, your topdog will probably try to kill your underdog. A dialogue, something like the following, will usually occur internally between your topdog and your underdog.

T: Well, dammit, you've done it again!

U: I'm sorry.

T: We were going to go back to school to get that MBA, but you forgot to check the calendar and we missed registration again.

U: I feel just terrible about it.

T: How are we going to get ahead if you keep screwing us up?

U: I'll try harder next time. I promise.

T: It's just like that short course we never completed, because you went ahead and got a head cold during the last three sessions.

U: Gimme another chance.

Even though the topdog is characterized by ambition, drive, and determination, and the underdog is characterized by whimpering, sniveling, and failure, it's the underdog who always wins! Your topdog is that part of you that gets you where you're going. It houses your capacity for endurance, competence, and effectiveness. It is the source of most of your successes and can be thought of as your base of power. The thing you must recognize is that your underdog also serves a vital function—it houses your resistance, which is another source of power.

Your underdog stops you from taking on too much, from overreaching your current level of effectiveness, and from committing yourself to things that are not in your best interest. It also keeps you alive in potentially threatening situations. For example, it's your topdog that is firmly committed to telling your boss off at the next staff meeting and your underdog that clamps your mouth shut at the very last minute.

There are a few individuals who have somehow managed to kill or to avoid responding to their underdog. These people are easily identifiable by certain behavior patterns. These are the people who confront every issue, head on, regardless of the risks or consequences. They start projects but rarely, if ever, consider the costs of these projects. Frequently they broadcast plans and expected outcomes long in advance of actually starting on the plans. These same people take huge and often unrealistic risks. And when a project fails, it is rarely, if ever, their fault in their eyes. Long on giving advice, for example, "If I were you, what I'd tell that bum is . . . ," they are usually short on giving support.

There are also some people who have effectively destroyed or neutralized their topdog. These people are also easily recognizable by certain chronic behaviors. The overriding characteristic is their tendency to go for the immediate, short-term benefit that requires the least effort. They tend to adopt the easiest, quickest, dullest path to get themselves off the hook. They take few, if any, risks and operate at a relatively low level of energy. They are also chronic self-pitiers.

The strategy for dealing with the topdog–underdog problem is not to have them in perpetual conflict but, instead, to have them work together.

T: We have to go back to school to get an MBA.
U: I don't want to go back.
T: Why not? It's essential to our success if we want to get a promotion and move up in the organization.
U: It's too much work. Besides, I'm afraid that we're not smart enough or that we don't have what it takes to get a master's degree.
T: How about if we sign up for just one course at the graduate level, just to see how we do?
U: Can it be a fun course?
T: Sure, just as long as it's relevant. Okay?
U: Okay.

Once you are clear that where you are heading is relatively safe and in your best interest, your tendency is to go ahead and get what you want. When you have honored your resistance and taken steps to actively avoid the needless risks and the things that you do not want to do, the tendency of your underdog is to *support* your topdog, rather than to perpetually subvert it.

Resistance As a Personal Asset

If you are among the many people who see resistance as a negative behavior, you probably see it that way when you want something from someone, rather than when you are being asked for something. Although, unfortunately, when you are being asked for something, you may buy into the view that something is wrong with you if you resist, and you may then begin to feel guilty or bad about yourself because of it. In terms of your well-being, resistance provides four clear benefits: Resistance protects you from being hurt or permanently damaged. Resistance guards your effectiveness. Resistance heightens your awareness of who you are. And resistance keeps you from being overstimulated.

Resistance Protects You from Being Hurt

A pervading myth of our time is that people resist change. I don't think that this is so. What I think is that people resist *pain*. In fact, I think what people really resist is the opposite of change, that is, boredom, which is one of the most painful things.

Very few people will actively look for situations that have the potential for causing them pain. It is your resistance that stops you from rushing headlong into actions or projects that have a potential for causing you harm. At times you may not even be aware of what the potential harm is, only that somewhere the potential exists. Your thought may be, "I can't put my finger on what's bothering me about this; all I know is that something doesn't fit or feel right about it for me." These "rumblings" are preverbal pieces of information that you are processing. I firmly believe that it is important for everyone to attend to and honor these indications of resistance. These signals can prevent you from getting yourself into a position that could eventually harm you—ethically, morally, socially, professionally, or psychologically. And simply by paying some attention to them, you are withholding immediate permission to go ahead with something that can, in the end, prove to be mildly painful or absolutely disastrous.

Resistance Guards Your Effectiveness

An overriding assumption coming out of the behavioral sciences over the past 20 years is that people have an inborn need to grow and to be effective and to avoid failure whenever possible. As an advocate of this assumption, I believe that very few people will take on a task or an objective willingly when the likelihood of failure is reasonably great.

As an example, a competing weightlifter may attempt a lift that is 5 pounds heavier than his most successful lift but will not attempt one that is 50 pounds heavier.

There is little question that your effectiveness is contingent upon your willingness to take risks and to try new and different challenges. All growth occurs at the boundary; however, that is also where all risk is located. Clarity about where the ultimate limit is, that is, the amount of risk you are willing to take, is essential to protecting your capacity to be effective. As you move closer to the outer edge, your resistance to further movement increases as well. Honoring your resistance not to take on a task or an objective that clearly exceeds the limits of your competence is every bit as essential to your effectiveness and success as is being willing to take on those challenges and responsibilities that stretch your limits.

Resistance Heightens Your Awareness of Who You Are

In Chapter 2, I said that your I-boundary is determined by where your subboundaries fall on all the various dimensions that define the human condition. By being aware of your values, tastes, and preferences, you can define and characterize yourself and in this way increase your self-awareness. And keep in mind that what you discount, avoid, or do not like is equally defining of you. For example, it is just as defining of me that I dislike wine as it is that I like ale. Thus you are as identifiable to yourself and to others by the things you resist as you are by the things you pursue.

Most individuals begin to develop some sense of what does and does not fit for them in the first years of life. But there is also a slow process that begins in children's formative years in which parents and the institutions children come in contact with act to positively reinforce the children's values and preferences to match theirs and denigrate and negatively reinforce those that do not. By the time children have reached young adulthood, most of them have learned to want and value what their parents and society say they should want and value and to resist what their parents and society say they should not want and value. In other words, the individuals can readily become confluent with the environmental influences that have been reinforcing their behaviors, either positively or negatively, over the years.

During this period, there are occasions when the individual resists the influences that are shaping his growth. This resistance contributes to his development by heightening his awareness of his personal boundaries. The process creates a very effective counter to confluence and all the elements of power loss that accompany confluence.

Resistance Keeps You from Being Overstimulated

An extremely important function of resistance is that it stop you from being inundated by the thousands of things that are occurring within and around you all the time. Take a moment to consider all the things that are happening right now that could command your attention—sights, sounds, smells, thoughts, and so on. It is easy to see that if you attempted to respond to each of these stimuli as it occurred, you would never get anything that is of value to you accomplished. Resistance allows you to block out the distractions that would otherwise keep you from concentrating on the thing that you wish to accomplish.

As resistance blocks the distractions from the physical environment, it also blocks distractions from the social and work settings. At times, resisting others' information or viewpoints can be as effective as listening to them. For example, it is very important to listen to why something won't work before you make a final decision. Once you have made your decision, however, listening to one more round of why it won't work is not only a bore but also an energy drain. An example that is a little closer to home is the usually correct accusation, "You haven't heard a word that I've said!" When I am guilty of this, it is very often because I am preoccupied with other matters that I feel are more pressing or because what is being said is somehow threatening to me. In either case, my resistance is protecting me.

One of the most functional forms of resistance is boredom. Where most forms of resistance keep you from being distracted from your objective by the many other stimuli in the environment, boredom keeps you from being distracted from your objective by a *single* source in the environment. Boredom gives you the simple message that you have had enough for right now; it performs the same service that a full stomach does when you are eating. Very few people will continue to eat or drink once they have reached their full capacity. On the other hand, many of these same people will continue an activity well past their point of tolerance.

Boredom is not a life style, nor is it an unavoidable aspect of living or of working. Boredom is merely a clear signal that deserves as much attention and respect as an upset stomach. Boredom does not necessarily indicate that what you are doing is unimportant or even unenjoyable. What it indicates is that for right now you have reached your capacity for this activity, and pursuing it any further at this time will result in increased discomfort and in no further accomplishment. Honoring your boredom does not imply that you should abandon an objective. It does suggest that you need a rest or a new approach if you are going to do the work well.

Some of the signals of boredom are fidgeting, restlessness, yawning, inability to focus your attention, daydreaming, and "nodding off." Should you become aware of any of these signals, try the following procedure as a way to deal with the boredom:

1. Take full responsibility for your own boredom. It is something that you do to you.
2. Recognize the signals and accept them for what they are.
3. Stop what you are doing.
4. Determine whether you need a rest or a new approach to the activity.
5. If you decide that you need a new approach, think of at least three alternatives for pursuing the objective. Choose and refine the one that generates the most energy and excitement in you.
6. If you cannot think of three alternatives or come up with a good alternative from among the three choices, take a break from the activity. Excuse yourself, work on something else that needs doing, take a walk, or watch a little TV. In other words, focus your attention on another activity.

These steps will interrupt your boredom and replenish your energy, so that you can go back and accomplish what you set out to do.

Resistance as an Organizational Asset

If an organization is going to grow and prosper, it is essential that, whenever possible, the needs of the individual be integrated with the needs of the organization. Just as resistance is an asset to an individual, it is also an asset to organizations. And once again, resistance provides some very clear benefits to the organization, including these: Resistance differentiates talent. Resistance provides new information. Resistance produces energy. And resistance makes the organization safe.

Resistance Differentiates Talent

Resistance allows the organization to identify and utilize the talents of its members more effectively. In most medium- to large-size families, it is not unusual for each child to be encouraged to develop the specific talents and areas of interest that best represent the child's strong points. One child may be encouraged to participate in an athletic program; another may be encouraged to take music lessons; and another may be an excellent student who is encouraged and coached on a science project. The rewards distributed correspond with the talent, for example, a catcher's mitt for the athlete, concert tickets for the young musician, and a chemistry set for the student. Individuality is stressed, usually within the context of a clear set of values concerning right and wrong and how people get along together in this family.

The payoffs accrue not only to each child, in terms of his or her development, but also to the family, in terms of the creation of an effective support system. Tolerance for and appreciation of difference are developed, and support is available in terms of skill swapping. For example, the student can suggest a viable research project to the athlete, who can coach the student on how to hit a longer ball.

The key to this development of individual effectiveness in the family is resistance—for example, "Just because my older brother loves the violin doesn't mean I do." Forcing a child to take up the violin, or anything else for that matter, when that child's resistance to it is running high will only result in an unhappy and resentful child and the tragic loss of potential talent in other areas.

Work organizations operate with the same dynamics as families; that is, the basic things that make a family effective also make a work organization effective. However, many organizations, even those that are honestly attempting to better the working relationships, have an unfortunate tendency to standardize rewards, to encourage conformity, to promote getting along well over being productive, and to view resistance as something to be stamped out. The worst thing that you can be accused of is not being a team player.

One of the biggest destroyers of effectiveness is an organizational norm that verbal resistance is no different from out-and-out refusal. That is, stating that a particular action may not be in the best interest of the organization is tantamount to refusing to do it and is often interpreted as an act of rebellion. A person who resists an assignment is almost always making *two* statements. The first, very clear, message is: "I don't want to do this." The second, tacit, message is: "There is something else I can do better." In most cases, when somebody says no to you, there is a yes hidden under the surface. For example, suppose I asked you, "Would you volunteer to be the United Way chairperson this year?" and you responded, "No." Your no is the first statement. If I then asked, "Okay, what would you like to volunteer for?" and you said, "Toys for Tots," there is a yes, or second statement. Although I recognize that you could also have responded by saying, "I don't want to volunteer for anything," that doesn't happen as often as you might think.

Resistance Provides New Information

Until you have reached a final decision, the more pertinent information that you have at your disposal, the better. One of the best ways to surface relevant information is to listen to what people who do not like the idea are saying. In fact, if the overall objective is commonly held, encouraging people to resist any particular approach to it provides a broader range of alternatives from which to choose. This can be easily and safely accomplished by assigning one individual at each meeting the role of "devil's advocate."

The wants of many individuals often emerge when they become aware of what they do not want. In other words, when you are clear about what you want to reject, it is frequently much simpler for you to figure out what would fit better for you; that is, it is always easier to go from one clear place to another clear place, than it is to go from no place to a clear place.

Another way in which resistance is a source of new information is that it surfaces potentially harmful outcomes. Because of a difference in value systems or perhaps because you are too close to the situation to be objective, another member of your organization may be better able to see some pitfalls or potentially disastrous outcomes. If this is the case, it is always much better to have this information out in the open as soon as possible.

Resistance Produces Energy

Human energy is as vital to the running of an organization as gasoline is to the running of a car. Of course, cars can coast for quite a distance, and so can most organizations. For an organization to maintain its vitality and growth, it must have a base of energy, excitement, and activity. Clearly a major source of this energy comes from actively pursuing goals and objectives. An often-neglected source of energy is the resistance of others.

For example, both a relay race and a tug-of-war have an objective to be met, concerted team effort is involved, and there is a clear indicator of success or failure. The only major difference between the two events is that in the relay race the energy is focused on advancing and in the tug-of-war it is focused on "pulling back." The most salient commonality between the two events is that both produce energy. The critical concern is to get the energy *surfaced*. Once the energy is up, it becomes a relatively easy task to channel it in productive directions.

I never have more energy available than when I am being dragged, kicking and screaming, to a place I would prefer not going to. If I am going along quietly, it is usually because I am using more energy stifling the resistance than I would probably use to actively and openly resist.

Resistance is the key variable that makes conflict a positive and usable force. Suppose that you and I are jointly committed to an organizational objective. I advocate one approach, via Plan A, and you advocate another approach, via Plan B. Assuming that we stay focused on the objective, the resulting conflict will be cast not only in terms of what we each want (power) but also in terms of what we do not want (power by way of resistance). Handled effectively, the energy and creativity that this conflict will produce are healthy and beneficial both for us and for the organization. We may end up creating an entirely new approach based on the ideas generated by the energy produced by our initial resistance to each other's method.

Resistance Makes the Organization Safe

Since not everything is good for everybody, when you know what is potentially harmful, you know what to avoid or resist. People will protect themselves as best they can, regardless of the circumstances in which they find themselves and regardless of who says they should or should not protect themselves. It is their resistance that protects them.

The most common organizational approach to dealing with resistance is to try to convince you that you should not feel resistant. An organization chooses this approach either because it sees resistance as counterproductive or because it believes resistance violates the norm for developing trust, caring, and teamwork.

When an organization supports the position that resistance is a liability, the result is usually only the *appearance* of good working relationships and cooperation. In most cases, these desirable attributes are being undercut by unexplained blockages within the system. That is, the resistance is still there, but it is being suppressed and is manifesting itself in other, more destructive ways. Energy that could be invested in organizational objectives is being displaced into political maneuvering, stating disagreement very diplomatically, or just sitting on anger and letting it fester, only to surface at a later time.

The other available alternative is to view resistance as an *asset* and to establish an organizational culture that values stating resistance openly and clearly. The effect will be that energy that was once being held in reserve for self-protection will now be used to attain objectives.

CHAPTER 6

Dealing with Resistance

Because most organizations and families see resistance as a negative force, almost all their approaches to resistance seem to focus on eliminating it. In the family, the strategies often *overemphasize* cooperation, playing nicely, and sharing. In the organization, training practices, such as T-groups, encounter groups, and sensitivity training, have been devised to promote the ideal of totally open communication among all unit members. The marathon, a 24-hour, nonstop encounter group, was specifically designed as a method for attacking individual defenses through the use of direct confrontation aided by the physical exhaustion that occurs as the hours go by. It is important to emphasize that these techniques can be valuable tactics if they are conducted to meet a situational need of an organization and its members and if they are conducted and led by properly trained and reputable leaders. It is only when these techniques and values become entrenched as dogma in a system that they become less useful and sometimes counterproductive.

From a personal viewpoint, resistance is very productive for me when I am resisting something that you want that I do not wish to give. Resistance is also beneficial to the organization when, say, one employee resists a poor decision made by another. At this point, an interesting observation emerges: That is, it is an altogether different matter when you resist something that I want from you. What we have here is an authentic double standard. That is, it is perfectly okay for me to resist you, but it is not all right with me, in most instances, for you to resist me. I may even respect your right to resist me, but I never have to like it! The same holds true for you. The question becomes: How do I effectively reduce or eliminate your resistance when it is blocking me from getting what I want?

To deal with resistance, you first must recognize it. In most cases, if resistance is present, it will be manifest in the first thing that is said by the resister after the demand has been made clear.

For example, suppose that Pete wants Charlie to put in some overtime on a project that is near completion.

> **P:** Charlie, I'd like you to stay a little later tonight so that we can finish up the Digby project.
>
> **C:** I'd love to help but I have a commitment this evening.

The very next thing said by Pete—his *initial* response to Charlie's resistance—will be the most important influencing factor in determining Pete's success in reducing Charlie's resistance. Pete's next statement will also set the stage for all subsequent communications pertaining to the issue.

Negative Approaches to Resistance

There are three traditional, basic strategies used to deal with other people's resistance: *breaking it down*, in which the resistance is attacked as soon as it begins to surface; *avoiding it*, in which the resistance is allowed to surface and then an attempt is made to sidestep it; and *minimizing it*, in which the resistance is allowed to surface and then an attempt is made to discount it.

Strategy 1. Breaking Down Resistance

Adherents of the traditional strategy of breaking down resistance have four obvious responses to resistance: to use ultimatums, threats, or coercion, to use a sales approach, to use an appeal to reason, and to use an appeal to basic values. A negative of all these responses is that even if you succeed in temporarily reducing or eliminating the immediate resistant behavior, you are still stuck with the resistance itself. The effects of the covert resistance will usually appear as reduced energy, decreased input, and minimal compliance with the demand. As you will see, each of these responses carries its own costs.

Ultimatums, Threats, Coercion. Ultimatums were briefly referred to in Chapter 1 as an example of a poor two-choice strategy. Ultimatums are also the most common, the least effective, and the most destructive technique for reducing resistance. The ultimatum is known for its "or else" at the end of a statement, used as a direct threat of force or sanction. Let's take a look at the effects of an ultimatum in an example that most of us have experienced either as participants or as observers, that is, when you tell a child, "You will sit there until you eat all your dinner, including your vegetables, or else!" The "or else" may have meant "no dessert" or "You'll go to bed hungry" or "You'll sit there until you do." There are many costs that accrue in such a situation.

Let's say your threat was "no dessert." In this situation, the child may (and more than likely will) begin to associate rewards with eating everything on the plate, which eventually roughly translates itself into "I'm not doing anything for you or for me unless I see a reward in the offing" (better known as immediate gratification), instead of associating a balanced meal with health and personal well-being (a reward in itself). The cost: inappropriate association of a behavior with a reward system. You both pay a price. You have to keep paying off, as will eventually the child's teachers and the child's employers. And the child will continue to expect a payoff, never understanding the intrinsic value of an activity. And in this instance, there is a possible secondary cost of an overweight child.

If your threat was "You'll go to bed hungry," and the child still chooses not to finish dinner, you have set yourself up for head-on confrontation (a lose/lose situation) in which you have to either carry out your threat of sending your child to bed hungry or back down from your threat (you lose/the child wins), at which time you also lose your credibility. Whichever way it goes, you lose because what you really want is for your child to eat a balanced meal. What you get instead is a hungry, angry, resentful, and probably more resistant child, who is beginning to associate mealtimes with punishment and who will eventually learn to test every threat you make to see whether or not you will carry it out. Also, if you are inconsistent, confusion sets in with the child along with inappropriate behaviors.

All this is equally true for the threat "You'll sit there until you do." In addition, I'm sure you can imagine what it must be like for the child left sitting alone at a table when everyone else has finished. Mealtimes become associated with loneliness and empty time to build up further anger and resentment. The very best you can hope for is that your child forces down the food while developing a lasting resentment for the food, mealtimes, and you, the enforcer of the rule.

Although frequently couched in more subtle and tactful terms, the ploys are quite similar in the work setting. Although on the surface threats and coercion *appear* to work in all settings, their result is in fact only minimal compliance with the demand and resentment felt toward the demand and the demander. The paradox is that a threat that appears to successfully eliminate resistance in reality creates even more and deeper resistance.

The Sales Approach. The prime assumption of the demander who uses a sales approach for breaking down resistance is: "If I can get Joe to really understand that what I want is good for him, he'll stop resisting and start supporting my demand." This is certainly a tempting assumption, but it is usually a wrong one.

First, Joe knows what is best for him. Second, if you are successful in momentarily shattering Joe's resistance, Joe ends up stuck with something he didn't really want, which will leave you facing much stiffer resistance the next time you face Joe.

As an example, the really professional sales rep is always after the account, not just the sale. During my years as a sales rep for an industrial maintenance concern, I insisted that customers return any item that they were not absolutely satisfied with. After all, they saw me only once every three weeks; they saw the manufacturer's label every time they went into the supply room.

The time to sell your idea is when you make the demand, *not* when the other person shows resistance. When you succeed in using selling to eliminate or reduce resistance, the resister has to live forever with the message: "I've been had," and you lose credibility and have to resell your idea each time resistance to your demand surfaces.

The Appeal to Reason. The appeal-to-reason approach to breaking down resistance is similar to the sales approach. The difference between the two is that in the sales approach you appeal to the resister's emotion, whereas in this approach, you appeal to the resister's reason. Here the demander's primary assumption is: "If my argument is more logical than your argument, I will automatically win." Although such thinking seems logical, the actual outcome is usually the opposite. Once you have tried to devastate me with your logic and to demonstrate that you are my intellectual superior, hell will freeze over before I support you!

During a recent workshop, I role-played a situation with a supervisor who was having a very difficult time getting the support she needed from a collague in personnel. After giving me some background information, Joanna played herself and I played the resistant personnel supervisor. The dialogue went like this:

J: I need you to complete the forms on time.
H: I'll try.
J: I want them by the end of this week.

H: I'm a little too busy right now to be able to promise that. I have too many other obligations at the moment.

J: What if I can prove that you are wrong?

Stop! At this point, Joanna lost. As soon as she delivered that challenge, the issue shifted from task completion to pure power confrontation. What I wanted most at that time was not to avoid the task but to save face.

No one likes to be made to feel foolish or inferior. Even when the content of the demander's request makes sense, if this method is used to obtain compliance, it will tend to increase the resister's resistance rather than decrease it.

The Appeal to Basic Values.   In this attack on resistance, you appeal to the resister's core values—loyalty, honor, courage, and so forth. If you are successful, the resister's self-esteem is diminished as a result of his resistance.

Remarks such as, "Where's your company loyalty?" "What are you trying to do—make points with the boss?" "What's the matter? Are you chicken?" tend to put the resister on the defensive. Should you succeed in getting the compliance in this way, be aware that you pay the price of having the resister see himself as being in a weaker position. People who see themselves as weak tend to focus on protecting themselves rather than contributing to others. The best they'll offer is temporary compliance, not cooperation. If, on the other hand, the resister sees your appeal as a direct personal attack on his values, his resistance is immediately increased and solidified.

There are two cautions to keep in mind when you attempt to break down someone's resistance. First, a person's overriding reaction to an attack on his resistance is to offer increased resistance; that is, the harder I push, the harder you will push back. The parents of any teenager will tell you that the surest way to solidify the relationship between your daughter and her current boyfriend is to criticize the boyfriend. Second, if you do succeed in breaking down an individual's resistance, remember this quote I once read on a wall poster: "Just because you have silenced a man does not mean that you have converted him."

Strategy 2.   Avoiding Resistance

Deflection, inflicting guilt, and appealing to the resister's self-interest are the three approaches most often used by demanders who employ the strategy of avoiding resistance.

Deflection. Deflection, in itself a form of resistance, is a technique in which you allow another's resistance to emerge and then you redirect it away from the target. There are many ways to deflect resistance. The simplest method is to ignore what the resister is saying and go on with what you are saying, as though the resister had not said anything in the first place. This forces the resister to interrupt you in order to restate the objection. If the resister persists, you can sometimes further block the objection just by glaring at him and going on with what you are saying.

Another common deflector is the phrase "Yes, but . . . ," used as soon as the resistance appears. For example, if I say to a salesperson, "This jacket doesn't hang right across my shoulders," and the response I get back is, "Yes, but isn't it a beautiful shade of blue?" my objection to the jacket has just been deflected. Changing the subject and intentionally misinterpreting the resistance are other forms of deflection.

No matter what form the deflection takes, the problems that can arise are the same: The resister experiences frustration and anger, and the deflector gets a reputation for being patronizing, for not hearing, or for confusing messages.

Inflicting Guilt. The guilt tactic often takes the form of a statement like "After all I've done for you" or "You can't let me down." A subtle variation is "That's okay, don't worry about me." The aim here is to make the resister feel ungrateful and therefore guilty of betrayal. Inflicting guilt can be a very powerful shaper of behavior; and if it is done skillfully and repeatedly, guilt can be implanted as a chronic element of the resister's personality.

A very old piece of advice to parents goes: If you want to make your son feel guilty, give him two shirts for his birthday—a red one and a blue one. If he wears the red one first, ask him, "What's the matter, don't you like the blue one?" If he wears the blue one first, ask him, "What's the matter, don't you like the red one?" This will produce guilt and confusion every time.

The problem with using inflicting guilt as a means of avoiding resistance is that it creates a lot of needless pain, often in people who care a lot about you. And if you use this method often, you'll end up with much weaker people supporting you than if you don't use this method.

Appealing to the Resister's Self-Interest. In this approach, you skirt the resistance by appealing to the resister's self-interest. Instead of responding to the resister's objection, you immediately point out what's in it for the resister if she goes along with you. The problem is that you do not surface the resistance, and it will be there to haunt you both even if the resister's compliance is forthcoming.

A variation of this tactic is the buy-off. In this case, you simply bribe the resister to withdraw by offering him a payoff that has nothing to do with the issue at hand. A risk that attends the buy-off is that if you misjudge the resister, he may consider your bribe an insult to his ethics or value system. This can be disastrous to your relationship. Or if the buy-off is successful, you may end up creating what I refer to as the "vicious cycle" effect; that is, if at a later date the roles are reversed, you may be put in the position of withholding your resistance in return for a future payoff from the former resister.

Strategy 3.   Minimizing Resistance

There are three ways to minimize resistance; by discounting it, by defusing it, and by appealing to unanimity.

Discounting Resistance.   A discounting response is used to minimize the emerging resistance so that the resistance appears trivial. There are several ways to accomplish this. One way is to initiate your response to the resistance with "You can't mean that . . . " and to paraphrase the objection back to the resister. For example, the resister says, "I don't think we can afford the move at this time," and you snicker and say, "You can't mean to tell me that you're going to let a few bucks get in the way?" This tactic is particularly effective when it is done publicly.

Another way is to take the resister aside and put your arm over his shoulder. Assume that he is no more capable of intelligent thought than the average 8-year-old and in one-syllable words explain that he just isn't getting the "big picture."

Defusing Resistance.   In defusing resistance, you anticipate the resistance and respond to it *before* the resister has a chance to express it. For example, "Claudia, I am sure you're going to squawk a bit at the price, but I think we need a larger computer." If you surface the resistance first and immediately discount it, the resister can rarely do more than acknowledge your statement. Even if the point of the resistance is legitimate, it has lost most of its impact.

The effect of this is much like saying to someone at a party, "Hey, Pete, tell them the one about the salesman who ends up on the iceberg with the duck." Once you have publicly identified the joke by its punchline, the teller is finished.

Appealing to Unanimity. In this approach to minimizing resistance, you make a virtue out of "togetherness." This is actually a strategy more than a tactic, in that the group constantly and consistently emphasizes the value of pulling together no matter what. In this type of organizational environment, any statement of resistance, particularly one dealing with the leader's wants, can be and often is interpreted as disloyalty to the group. This results in the resister's constantly being in jeopardy of being seen as a threat to the group's well-being. In organizations where there is an overemphasis on the value of togetherness, the statement of resistance will place the resister—rather than the object of his resistance—under suspicion.

Some early indicators of this condition are a motion for unanimous support after a split vote; statements like, "I'm sure that we all agree that . . . ," and appeals to group identity, as in "We all feel that . . . , right?"

The appeal to unanimity as a way of dealing with resistance is probably the most destructive to group effectiveness, since it is one of the prime producers of confluence. The results of this are that team playing becomes more important than winning and the individual is valued more for loyalty than for competence.

An additional cost of all tactics geared to minimizing resistance is that the resisters are presented as being weak, petty, or stupid. If and when the resisters start to see themselves this way, they do begin to resist less; however, they also tend to contribute a lot less across the board.

Conclusion

Although these traditional, low-yield strategies for dealing with resistance do sometimes work, they support the erroneous assumption that resistance is bad for the individual and for the group. Even when they are used successfully, they generally provide only a temporary solution at best and are quite costly in terms of developing a more human system in which to live and work. Used unsuccessfully, these low-yield strategies generally create resistance that is greater and deeper than the original resistance that they were designed to eliminate.

Note that there will be times when some of these responses to resistance will be quite appropriate, such as in a crisis situation. Also, some of these responses are not dysfunctional in and of themselves, for example, appealing to reason, to self-interest, or to the common good. They are destructive when used in inappropriate situations and as the initial response to someone's resistance. As a general approach, however, I suggest that these strategies be avoided, since there is a better way to go.

The Positive Approach to Resistance

There are two basic assumptions that I want to reinforce that are central to dealing creatively with resistance. The first assumption is that resistance *is* and will always be. People will always resist, knowingly or unknowingly, those things that are not in their best interest. The second assumption is that resistance needs to be honored and dealt with respectfully. If it is handled from this perspective, resistance becomes an organizational asset and it can develop, rather than injure, the relationship between the demander and the resister.

The strategy that I advocate for dealing with resistance creatively has four steps: surfacing, honoring, exploring, and rechecking. You must complete each step before moving on to the next step.

Before we go into the positive strategy for dealing with resistance, I want to mention one precondition that is absolutely essential if the work is to be successful: *You must be crystal clear about what it is that you want from others.* The resistance that is expressed can only be as clear as the demand to which it is directed. It is incumbent upon you to be as clear as you can about what you want and to be specific when expressing your want to another person. The more you can express your demand in terms of time frames, specific outcomes, potential benefits, and concrete behaviors that are needed, the higher the probability that you will get agreement if it is available or *clear, workable* resistance if agreement is not available.

Step 1.   Surface the Resistance

After you have clearly stated what it is you want from another person, the first, and probably the most difficult, step is to get out in the open whatever resistance the other person has. Many people will withhold their resistance for a variety of reasons. For instance, if there has been a past history of experiencing a heavy emphasis on the low-yield strategies, particularly on breaking down resistance, the resisters may feel highly vulnerable. After all, they have been told for a long time that it is not good or appropriate to be resistant; and now it suddenly becomes okay. Some mistrust about the okayness is more than likely going to occur initially. In many cases, the individuals may not be aware of how, or even of what, it is that they are resisting. Regardless of the reasons, or their legitimacy, most people will surface only those things that it is safe for them to disclose. What this suggests is that it may take some time to develop the level of trust needed to get at and surface all the relevant issues. Don't expect to get it all the first time! The surfacing of resistance can be approached easily and effectively by keeping these guidelines in mind:

1. *Make it as safe as you can.* State clearly, publicly if possible, that you want to hear the resistance. Be sure to include why it is imporant to you and be as straightforward as possible—for example, "Here is what I want. Do you see any potential problems?" Recognize that in the initial attempt there will probably be some early testing of you. That is, some of the resistance that you hear may be designed to test your reaction, rather than to deal with the issue at hand. This is the place for control and *simple acceptance* of what is being said. Do not counterattack! When the resisters are aware that you are not going to counterattack or try to sell them, you stand a much better chance of getting at the real resistance. For example, an open expression of a resister's mistrust of you personally, should that be the case, is an excellent first step. Now you know where you stand with that person and what you have to overcome, which gives you a good beginning to deal with the issue at hand. Again, keep your cool and go slowly! It takes time to build trust.

2. *Ask for all of it.* Listening to what people tell you about what they do not like about you or about what you want is rarely a pleasurable experience. Nevertheless, since these feelings are there anyway, it is in your best interest to get out all that you can. It is okay to probe the resistance as it is being expressed as long as you do it gently. The tendency to feel defensive and to want to counterattack will be there. Once again, do not give in to these feelings. If the resister has responded incorrectly to something because of a misinterpretation of your statement, it is perfectly appropriate for you to restate your original position so that it is clearly understood. Do no more than this, however, at this time.

I find it very helpful to write down the resistances as they are being stated out loud. This way I don't miss anything. Also, nothing will be forgotten since I needn't rely on my memory. At the same time, I honor the resister. By writing down his words, I am letting him know that they are very important to me.

Step 2. Honor the Resistance

There are three phases to honoring the resistance: listening, acknowledging, and reinforcing.

1. *Listen to the resistance.* A point was made earlier that there is a

time for everything. There is a time for listening and there is a time for not listening. This is definitely one of the times to listen! When people are stating their resistance openly, they are providing you with two vital sources of information. First and most important to you, the person is giving you information about something that you want and about where some of the pitfalls to obtaining it may be. Second and most important to the resister, he is making a personal statement about who he is. Any attempt on your part to discount the information will not only stop the information from coming in but will also carry the clear message to the resister that his opinions don't matter very much and, therefore, neither does he.

It is crucial at this point to make no attempt to reinforce your original position, to sell, to reason, or in any way to imply that the other person should not feel the way he feels. *Just listen!*

2. *Acknowledge the resistance.* Acknowledging is really a part of listening and is the only means the resister has available to know that what he is saying is being heard. Acknowledging is done through eye contact, by occasionally restating a point that the resister has made, or by asking questions about the point that the resister is now making. Be authentic. Just as being defensive or reacting hostilely to the resister will stop the process, so will being patronizing or solicitous to the resister. When you acknowledge the resistance, you are communicating to the resister that you take seriously what he is saying, and you are also promoting a more productive relationship.

The act of acknowledgment in no way implies that you agree or disagree with the point being made by the resister. You are acknowledging the other person's right to resist openly and to feel whatever he feels at the moment. A statement such as "I understand how this could be a problem for you," "You certainly have a right to feel concerned," or "I was not aware of this aspect" allows you to respond to the resister's concerns without giving anything away; that is, if it is done sincerely.

Unless you honestly agree with the resister's point, avoid making any statements that reinforce the resistance itself. For example, if the resister says, "Wouldn't you agree that . . . ?" you can safely counter with "I understand how you could see it that way" without committing yourself to supporting the resistance that you want to see diminished. Don't give the store away! And remember that you want to hear this and you need the information.

3. *Reinforce the okayness of resisting.* Keep in mind that openly resisting in a safe environment may be a new experience for some individuals. There will probably be some overstating or understating of

resistance until the resister is more comfortable with and trusting of the new approach. It is important that you reinforce the okayness of resisting periodically. When a resister overstates a position with hostility, a response from you of "I can see and understand how come you're angry" is much more effective than yielding to the impulse to counterattack. Allow for the possibility of being personally abused. And maintain your control if this should occur. You do not have to sit back and take the abuse, but you do not want to create an attack/counterattack situation. With a firm and controlled statement, make it clear that personal abuse will not be tolerated and that it is disruptive to what you are both trying to accomplish. After you've made this point, get back to the original issue and the resistance to that issue. It costs very little to maintain control of the situation.

When you believe that someone is understating his resistance, a statement such as "It's really okay not to like all of this" will go a long way toward helping the resister become more open and comfortable with you.

Step 3. *Explore the Resistance*

It is in this step that the resister releases the energy he has expended to needlessly protect himself, and makes it available to the demander.

1. *Address the nature of the resistance.* When the resister is aware that he is safe and he is willing to openly discuss the resistance with you, it is time to explore the nature of the resistance together. The thrust here is to have the resister state his concerns as specifically and concretely as possible.

There are two varieties of resistance that have to be addressed: pseudo resistance and authentic resistance. Pseudo resistance is resistance that has nothing to do with the issue at hand. It is in response to conditions and attitudes that are usually grounded in the resister's past. A few examples are a general mistrust of people, a cynical view of life, bad interpersonal relationships, resentment of any authority, a hunger to make a personal impact, a fear of obligating himself, and, sometimes, being chronically unclear about what he wants. Authentic resistance, by contrast, is a statement of strength by the individual and is specifically directed at the situation at hand.

The first objective in exploring resistance is to be able to determine whether it is pseudo or authentic resistance. Once this is accomplished, the pseudo resistance can be set aside as irrelevant for the time being and the authentic resistance can be addressed directly.

2. *Probe the resistance.* In exploring resistance with the other person, two general questions are very useful in getting concrete information. The first is: "What is your objection?" And the second is: "What would you prefer?"

The first probe, "What is your objection?" forces the resister to respond specifically in terms of the demand. If the resister's response is vague or stated in generalities, for example, "It doesn't seem fair," or "I just don't know if it will work," you need to probe further, by asking, for example, "What tells you this?" With this type of firm but gentle probing, either you'll get a clear statement of authentic resistance or the resister will realize that the objection is pseudo resistance and will let it go.

The second probe, "What would you prefer?" puts the resister in a proactive position rather than in a reactive position. Holding back resistance requires a markedly greater amount of energy than does expressing it openly. When the other person realizes that you are not going to push, sell, or coerce, all the energy that he held in reserve to fend you off becomes free floating and available. In response to your question, the resister is now working *with* you toward reaching your objective, rather than using his energy to block or divert you. What you are now getting is alternative approaches to your demand, and you have paved the way to make it easier for the other person to give you what you want.

When all the resistance available has been surfaced, acknowledged, and explored and both you and the resister are aware of what the resister does and does not like about the demand, it is okay to explore the positive aspects of the demand. You can do this by asking other probing questions, for example, "What do you like about the proposal?" and "How could this proposal benefit you or your unit?" When you probe it's a good idea to stay away from "Why" questions, since they have a tendency to draw defensive responses. Introduce your probe questions with "What" and "How"; these will tend to focus the energy on the issue at hand, instead of creating any need for the individual to justify his opinions or attitudes. Also, avoid the leading questions "Don't you think . . . ?" as it puts you back into a position of selling the demand.

Step 4. Recheck

At the end of each meeting, after all the relevant demands and resistances have been surfaced, a brief recheck to establish where you and the other person are *now* in terms of the issue will help pull the discussion together. This is a necessary step, given the high probability that perceptions, both the resister's and yours, have changed to some degree. Carrying out this final step ensures that there is a clear understanding among all involved about what is to be done and what can be expected in terms of support and specific behaviors. Do not expect the resister to no longer resist if there has been no modification of the demand to accommodate his concerns. What you can expect is that the resistance, although still there, will not have its previous blocking force and, even if it has not diminished appreciably, will not increase. This expectation is also reasonable in situations where demands are made and there are no options for modification, for example, a new corporate policy, safety regulation, or law.

Ideally, by using this approach, you will always be able to remove all the resistance to what you want, and maintain warm working relationships throughout. Although this is not impossible, the more realistic and attainable objective is to be able to reduce the authentic resistance to a workable level so that the resister, although still not liking the demand, at least won't block it and may even be willing to contribute to a certain degree.

Conclusion

This approach to dealing with resistance has universal application. It can be used effectively in any situation where resistance is an issue, for example, conflict management, training or educational situations, and raising children. In one of my current training workshops, the first morning session is devoted to the subjects of conflict and power, and the first afternoon session is devoted to the topic of resistance. At the start of the afternoon session, I ask each individual to answer the question, "On a scale of one to ten, to what extent am I resisting this program?" And then I ask the group to break up into subgroups of three. The subgroups have ten minutes to work up a list of all the things they dislike about what I have said so far and about me personally. I then ask a member of each subgroup to read the group's list aloud to me. It's always surprising to see how willing most groups are to do this. I listen, acknowledge, and ask for clarification when needed. That's all I do at this time. When all subgroups have read their lists, I ask them to generate a similar list of all the things that they like about what I said and about me personally. Again, a member of each subgroup reads the list aloud to me. And again, I only listen and acknolwedge. As a final step, I address the total group and ask each person to individually review his or her list of "don't likes." I then ask each member to, once again, rate his or her present level of resistance on a scale of one to ten.

At no time during these sessions has there ever been an increase and in approximately 20 percent of the sessions there has been a decrease in resistance to what I am saying or to me personally. Along with other benefits already mentioned, this process provides me with the additional advantage of now being in better contact with the people I'm working with.

As with any alternative, there are clear costs and benefits associated with the positive approach to dealing with resistance. The costs are: It is time consuming. It requires good listening skills. And it can be very frustrating, particularly in the early stages. The benefits are: It separates pseudo from authentic resistance. It produces end results that you can see and count on. It builds solid working and interpersonal relationships. It establishes realistic norms for behavior. It produces more alternatives. And it is much easier on both you and the resister.

Common Expressions of Resistance and Creative Counters

There is simply no end to the ways in which resistance can be expressed, both verbally and behaviorally. What follows are some of the more common expressions of resistance along with creative counters. Keep in mind that when authentic resistance is expressed, it is usually to protect the resister, *not* to attack the demander.

Resistance: The Block
Expression: "I don't want to" or "I'd rather not."
Comment: The block is the cleanest form of authentic resistance and the easiest to work with. When a resister says, "No," or "I'd prefer not to," he is pretty clear about what the demander wants and where he stands in relation to it.
Counter: "What is your objection?" or "What would you prefer?"

Resistance: The Rollover (aka, Passive Resistance)
Expression: "Tell me *exactly* what you want me to do."
Comment: Whereas the Block is the most obvious form of resistance, the Rollover is one of the least obvious and therefore one of the most difficult to identify and work with. Frequently the resister doesn't even know that she is resisting. Passive resistance usually occurs in response to a fear of punishment by the demander; in other words, the resister feels that open resistance will be dealt with harshly. Passive resistance is expressed by minimal compliance with the letter of the demand and no compliance whatsoever with the spirit of it.

The most confounding aspects of passive resistance are that you often perceive it as compliance to your demand and you can't criticize it because it is expressed in terms of compliance (though minimal) with what you are asking for. When a passive resister says, "Tell me *exactly* what you want," you had better tell her *exactly* what you want, because that is all that you are going to get.

Counter: "This is exactly what I want you to do [be specific at this point]. Are you clear about what is being asked of you and what constitutes good performance?" This forces the resister to acknowledge the spirit of the demand and to shoulder responsibility for its fulfillment, not just for her own actions.

Resistance: The Stall

Expression: "I'll get on it first thing next week."

Comment: It is sometimes difficult to distinguish between a Stall and an honest response based on current conditions. Knowing how the person usually responds to requests or demands will help you make the distinction. That is, if he is usually cooperative and if the time he says he needs is not unreasonable, it is probably a positive response and not resistance. However, if he has a history of stalling, you need to deal with his response as resistance. The counter here will help you clarify the situation and break through resistance if it is being offered.

Counter: "Is there anything of a serious nature that would prevent you from starting on this tomorrow?"

Resistance: The Reverse

Expression: "Wow! What a great idea!"

Comment: The Reverse is a very subtle form of resistance and is practically impossible to identify without knowing the resister. The Reverse appears as a statement of enthusiastic support, when what you were expecting from this individual was a tough time. The Reverse is immediately followed up by the Stall. Although it appears that this person is very enthusiastic about the demand, she never really does anything about it. In effect, she tells you what you want to hear and then forgets about your demand as she walks out of your office.

This form of resistance is analogous to a bluefish that has just been well hooked. After fighting against the rod, the fish will suddenly reverse its direction and swim toward the rod faster than you can reel, in order to create the slack that it needs to spit the lure. The clue that a Reverse may be occurring is your finding yourself surprised by this individual's eager support.

Counter: "I'm really pleased that you like this proposal. What I would like right now is to hear all the specific aspects that you feel so positive about."

Resistance: The Sidestep
Expression: "Let Mikey try it."
Comment: The Sidestep is probably heard most frequently in the home setting, yet it pervades the work setting as well. It is expressed as a counterdemand to get someone else to do what you want. The appeal is to your sense of fairness, for example, "How come you didn't ask Chuck to do this?" If the resister is successful, you are now on the defensive and have to justify your choice. Teenagers are absolute masters of this technique, which is an outgrowth of the universal cry for justice: "It's not faaiirrrr!"
Counter: "I'm aware of your concern about Chuck's workload. I have some other things planned for him," *or* "He's already working on something I need done. In the meantime, what I'd like from you is. . . ."

Resistance: The Projected Threat
Expression: "Margaret won't like this."
Comment: Here the resistance is expressed in terms of an implied threat that someone else with some power won't approve of your demand. The fact is that the third party's view may or may not be positive, but no matter what, that view will be somewhat different from the resister's assumptions of what it will be. In any case, it is a separate issue and should not be dealt with here.
Counter: "I appreciate your concern and will check it out with Margaret. In the meantime, what I would like you to do is. . . ." *Or* "I'll bear that in mind. Now what objections do *you* have to doing this?"

Resistance: The Press
Expression: "You owe me one."
Comment: The Press is authentic resistance. In this situation, the resister does not want to do what you are asking him to do and is calling in an old debt to get off the hook. Depending on the situation, it may be perfectly acceptable to honor his resistance and clear the books. The important thing to keep in mind is that it is *your* decision as to whether or not this is an appropriate time to pay back the debt. If it is not, acknowledge the debt, which was incurred under different circumstances, and state that you would like him to respond to what is happening now.

Counter: "I realize that I owe you one; however, I need your help right now and would like to carry the debt a little while longer."

Resistance: The Guilt Trip
Expression: "See what you're making me do!"
Comment: The use of guilt is a common tactic in attempting to shape behavior. The essence of guilt is based on the erroneous assumption that we are all responsible for each other's welfare. There are certainly situations in which this is quite valid, for example, when the responsibility has been clearly contracted for, as in an apprentice training program, or when there is a relationship based on the assumption of responsibility, such as an older brother looking out for a younger brother. However, in the day-to-day situation of living and working together, the sounder assumption is that I am capable of taking care of me and you are capable of taking care of you. If this is not the case, we can let each other know. The cry "See what you are making me do!" is an appeal to you to disregard your own welfare in favor of the resister's. Keep in mind that the resister's problem with what you want is her problem, not yours. It's good for you to work with her problem but not to shoulder it.
Counter: "I'm sorry that this is a problem for you; however, what I want you to do is . . . ," *or* "I recognize that you would prefer not to do this. I'll take full responsibility for the demand. Now what I want is.
. . ."

Resistance: The Tradition
Expression: "This isn't the way we've done it," or "We've always done it the other way."
Comment: This form of resistance is probably the most time-honored of them all. The traditional approach should not be summarily ignored or passed over simply because it has become a tradition. Sometimes the old way is the best way. Usually, however, the appeal of tradition is really an appeal to safety, not effectiveness, and a statement of a preference for mediocrity. Most individuals who rely heavily on traditional approaches are unwilling to take intelligent risks and have a low opinion of their own creativity and resourcefulness.
Counter: "I understand the value of the traditional approach; however, this situation is unique." *Or* "I agree that the old approach has some merit. What do you think we can do to adapt it to this new situation?"

Resistance: The Frontal Assault

Expression: "Has anyone ever told you what a jerk you are? Your next good idea will be your first one!"

Comment: If you have been dealing with resistance authentically, and if you have been acknowledging the dignity of the resister throughout, there is little chance of this occurring. However, every once in a while, a personal attack may occur. When a resister makes a personal attack on you, there are several things to keep in mind. First, the resister has lost control of the situation. Second, if you are the superior, the resister has placed himself in jeopardy. And third, there is clearly some resistance either to you or to the demand through you.

When you deal with resistance creatively, the strategy is always to maintain control. If you counterattack or invade the resister, you lose control of the process, particularly if there are others present. The meeting becomes a shouting match of insults and threats. If you become confluent with the resister and ignore the attack, you tell the resister and others that you have no right to dignity, and the resister takes over. The tactic, therefore, is to be contactful, which means that you take the shot at you and then tell the resister how you feel about what has just happened and what you want. There are an infinite number of contactful responses, depending on the nature and the depth of the attack. If the attack is so personal or abusive that any response would block the meeting, call a break and deal with the resister privately before continuing discussing your original demand. A personal attack may be dealt with playfully, sternly, inquiringly, or in other ways that you may think of, but it may never be ignored or used as a springboard for brutalizing.

Counters:

Playful: "Everyone has told me that! Now what don't you like about the idea?"

Stern: "I don't understand and, frankly, don't like your attack. I do not address you in that manner, nor will I tolerate being addressed in that way!"

Inquiring: "Apparently you are upset with me and with the idea. I would like to talk with you about what is going on with you after the meeting."

Conclusion

The ability to resist is a powerful part of the human makeup. It is neither good nor bad; rather it is a capacity that can be used to further strengthen individuals, families, and organizations. Individuals are never stronger or more creative than when they are resisting something that they perceive to be harmful. If people are going to become stronger and better able to contribute to their families and organizations, the first thing they must do is to realize that they already are strong and do have the ability to take care of themselves and to protect those things that are of most value to them.

CHAPTER 7

Resistance to Appropriate Behavior

Other people's resistance, whether authentic or pseudo, is a source of frustration and blockage to your getting what you want from the environment. The situations and examples discussed in Chapter 6 focused specifically on how to get more of something that someone else at first doesn't want to give you. The focus of working the resistance was on an objective. Working with resistance involves three elements: the demander (D), the resister (R), and the objective or thing wanted (O). For example, Pat (D) wants Jerry (R) to help on a project (O), or you (D) want your child (R) to get better grades (O).

In dealing with resistance to objectives, the issue is *productivity*. That is, you want a measurable outcome and the subordinate is resisting it. There are two reasons why dealing with resistance to objectives or work standards, however they are measured, is not too difficult. First, if someone's work or productivity drops off, there are usually clear and observable indications, for example, productivity is down by 4 percent, waste is up by 6 percent, or your kid's grades have dropped from two As and three Bs to two Bs, two Cs and a D. In these cases, it is relatively easy for you to state your demand in terms of the work standard or objective, which is external and can be seen clearly and objectively by both parties—for example, "The printout indicates that you're running behind schedule. What's the matter?" In effect, what you are looking at and hoping to alter are *nonproductive* behaviors.

Second, because there is an external standard, the resistance can be handled in an impersonal way. For example, you can address the person's use of time, method of operation, or study habits; and you need never mention the person's value system or personality characteristics in the process.

There is a second variety of resistance that occurs less frequently than nonproductive behavior but that is much more difficult to handle. This is the resistance that is directed against group norms or standards and that is expressed as *inappropriate* behavior. Of course, inappropriate behavior is a problem in itself, but it is also strongly related to nonproductive behavior.

Such things as chronic lateness, absenteeism, abusive behavior, flagrant violation of dress or conduct standards, and offensive personal habits all tend to tear at the fabric of normalized working relationships and put added and unnecessary stress into the work setting. This stress causes irritation and confusion, which can result in energy and commitment being drawn away from productivity. If inappropriate behavior is left unchecked, the consequence is usually a blurring of the standards of appropriate behavior and managers' feeling powerless and out of control.

Inappropriate behavior is more difficult to deal with than nonproductive behavior because of two factors. First, in situations of inappropriate behavior, there is a clear element of personalization that does not exist in situations of nonproductivity. Second, in inappropriate behavior situations, you as manager have to tackle personal issues and your own resistance to dealing with the matter *before* you confront the offending party.

Some questions that plague managers are: "Should I call it to Doug's attention now, or wait and hope that he will catch it without my having to say anything?" "If I raise the issue, will I offend Carol personally?" "Does Tim's action *really* constitute an offense?" "Is this particular issue really any of my business?" "Will Roberta feel overly guilty if I bring this up?" "Will my working relationship with Bob suffer if I confront him?" "Will Rae and others see me as a petty nitpicker if I raise the issue?" These are only a few of the very real concerns that managers struggle with and frequently stumble over as they attempt to deal with inappropriate behaviors in the work setting.

All too frequently, consultants and counselors rush in with quick-fix strategies or formulas to help the managers deal with these behavior problems, when what managers actually need first is an understanding of the problem.

Some Causes of Inappropriate Behavior

Most managers, supervisors, and parents tend to see inappropriate behavior as a problem to be simply and summarily stopped. What needs to be appreciated is that, more often than not, it represents an opportunity to coach or train the person to behave more appropriately.

Lack of Awareness

In many instances, the individual is simply not aware that the behavior in question is inappropriate or not in conformance with an established norm. This is sometimes the case with newly hired employees or with people who are transferred in from other locations. The best approach here is to inform the individual or to make sure that the orientation program covers the standards and norms for appropriate behavior in this department or organization. In terms of dollars and aggravation, it is always far less expensive to train people first than it is to try to change them later on. The rule of thumb is: If you have expectations for other people's behavior, inform them. If you have not informed them, their noncompliance is *your* responsibility.

Inappropriate Rule or Policy

Sometimes when inappropriate behavior occurs, it is the rule or policy that doesn't make much sense. Suppose there is an unwritten law that all employees are expected to attend every function sponsored by the organization regardless of their own needs or preferences. In some cases, the organization is attempting to enforce an unreasonable standard, but usually the rule or standard has lost its relevance as a result of changes in the environment and culture. Some examples are enforcing a strict dress code in an environment that has become more casual, attempting to regulate off-hour activities, and basing policies on managerial prerogatives rather than on prevailing conditions. What was considered very appropriate in the 1930s is unlikely to be applicable in the 1980s or 1990s. If an infraction occurs that is not really harming anything or anyone, the first thing to question is the rule, not the individual. To illustrate, when Eric was 4, one of our family rules was that on Saturday mornings he could get up early, get himself a bowl of cereal, and watch TV quietly until his mother and I came downstairs. What he couldn't do was leave the house. One Saturday morning, as I was coming down the stairs, Eric was coming in the front door. We saw each other at the same instant and he was was so scared, he literally could not speak. I bellowed, *"Where were you?"* and all he could manage to do was tremble violently and point to the bookcase. On the bookcase was a message in crayon that read, "I'm at Mrs. Anderson's." Mrs. Anderson was his neighborhood surrogate grandmother, and he had gotten bored and gone over to visit. Rather than yell at or punish him, I apologized. Clearly, he had taken a gutsy risk, not only in breaking an established rule, but in doing it openly and, most of all, responsibly. The fault had been mine for keeping in effect a rule that had stopped being useful.

Error in Judgment

No matter how effective you are on the job, or how "savvy" you may be in dealing with other people, every once in a while you're going to miss a signal, as did a friend of mine when he interpreted the word *informal* on a dinner invitation to mean slacks and sweater when what it meant was a suit and a tie. The worst thing that you can do in such a situation is to put too much emphasis or judgment on the offender; the best thing you can do is simply point out the mistake or gaffe and have a quick anecdote ready about how you once blew it.

Self-Interest

Sometimes a person behaves inappropriately because she gets more out of this behavior than she would get from behaving appropriately, as when the work is boring and an employee considers it worth the risk of getting caught showing up late or being chronically absent. Another example occurs when a good worker who has never been a problem suddenly realizes she isn't getting the recognition she deserves from management and she begins to mess up or be otherwise inappropriate on the assumption that if the manager won't recognize positive behaviors, maybe negative behaviors will catch his attention. A third example is the situation in which the offending individual is getting more peer respect for fighting the system than for helping to make it work.

Managers would do well to keep in mind that subordinates demand more from the work setting than just their paycheck at the end of the month. Many people are startled when they realize that adults spend more of their waking hours in the work setting than they do in any other single location, including their homes. Along with the paycheck and good working conditions, people need challenging work, responsibility, recognition for achievement, and a chance to grow and to increase their competence. If these needs are ignored or taken lightly, the result will not only be a loss of productivity, but also a high probability of increased inappropriate behaviors. If you as my manager choose to ignore my growth needs, I can respond in one of three ways.

I can submit to the conditions as they are. I can do whatever I can to avoid them. Or I can find ways to have some fun that you will probably interpret as nonproductive or inappropriate. In attempting to deal with inappropriate behaviors, you need to get a feel for the root cause of the offense before taking action. In some cases, you will find that you've had a hand in setting the conditions that resulted in the infraction.

Indirect Resistance

Sometimes inappropriate behavior is an expression of indirect resistance. In this case, the behavior contains a hidden message to be deciphered. That is, the offender is intentionally disregarding the signals for appropriate behavior because he wants to draw your attention to an even larger or more important issue. For example, the individual may want to get even, to stir up the system, or to make you look bad because of past injustices. In such an instance, the inappropriate behavior is a symptom of a much deeper problem. Indications that there is a deeper problem are (1) the offender is a chronic behavior problem, and (2) the relationship between you and the offender has been poor for a long time.

Authentic Resistance

Inappropriate behavior that is an expression of authentic resistance may occur when the rule or standard is appropriate but the individual has made a conscious, personal choice that it is *not* appropriate for him. Examples are not keeping your jacket on during working hours, not attending a company dinner, and not adhering to safety regulations when there is no apparent danger. As discussed earlier, if handled contactfully, authentic resistance is the most productive to work with since it can surface some useful information about the individual, his attitudes, and the situation that can be used to permanently remove the problem. In the case of authentic resistance, the working relationship between the manager and the subordinate is usually a good one.

Dealing with Inappropriate Behavior

There are two approaches to dealing with inappropriate behavior, regardless of its source: the judicial approach and the contactful approach. No matter which you use, the outcome will carry implications that extend far beyond the resolution of the incident at hand.

The Judicial Approach

The judicial approach is characterized by the phrase "Gotcha!" Here the manager's primary role is as judge and enforcer. The aim is to protect the rule or standard, and the strategy is to discipline the violator. The infraction is generally looked upon as an act of defiance against the organization and its management or is seen as a statement of nonconcern on the part of the offender. When the manager ends the session with the statement "Don't ever let me catch you doing that again!" the rules of the game have been redefined. The subordinate's payoff is now not for appropriate behavior but, rather, for not getting caught being inappropriate.

The Contactful Approach

The contactful approach is characterized by its problem-solving emphasis. Here the manager's primary role is as supporter of appropriate and/or effective behavior. The infraction is viewed as a specific event with its own set of causes and circumstances. The primary concern here is for the individual and how she interacts with the organization.

Here are several other distinctions between the two approaches.

Judicial	*Contactful*
Manager relies on authority.	Manager relies on power.
Working relationship is antagonistic.	Working relationship is collaborative.
Rule is often arbitrary.	Rule reflects reality.
Subordinates submit.	Subordinates cooperate.
Compliance increases resistance to the rule.	Compliance reduces resistance to the rule.
The result is temporary.	The result is permanent.
Compliance is minimal.	Compliance is optimal.

Guidelines for Dealing with Inappropriate Behavior

It seems apparent that taking a more contactful approach to dealing with inappropriate behavior would be beneficial to the manager, in terms of both specific outcomes and ease of attaining the desired behavior. The first step in addressing a situation involving inappropriate behavior is to ascertain whether the behavior is due merely to a lack of awareness or an error in judgment. In either case, a simple supportive reminder is all that is usually required. The last thing you want to do is to make more of the incident than is necessary. If the inappropriate behavior is due to any of the other causes, or if the cause is unclear, then the overall strategy is to help the person to see clearly that there is more to be gained from working with you than from working against you.

Regardless of how you choose to conduct the interaction, there are several guidelines to keep in mind when dealing with this situation.

*Deal with the Behavior, **Not** the Person.*   As mentioned before, one of the most frustrating and failure-producing endeavors that you can ever undertake is to attempt to change someone. This is particularly so when the someone is yourself. (Again, think about how many New Year's resolutions you ever really kept.) The moment that you take issue with someone's attitudes, beliefs, or values, you are implying that there is something wrong with that person in terms of who he or she is. I can almost guarantee that this will vastly increase the person's resistance to you personally and to giving you what you want. The truth is that regardless of your personal opinion, there is nothing wrong with the person. What is wrong is that an inappropriate *behavior* has occurred, and this can be dealt with in terms of the specific situation.

Be Specific.   Statements like "You have a bad attitude," "You're too abrasive," and "You don't take enough interest in your work" are all very general and can be interpreted as a direct attack on the individual. If that is how you are perceiving the situation, take the time to get in touch with *what* tells you that the attitude is bad, that the person is too abrasive, or that the person doesn't take enough interest in his work. Remember that it is the specific behavior that you want changed. You can best pursue this by supportively confronting your subordinate with what happened, when it happened, and how it affected his work. A statement such as "I'd like to talk with you about several occurrences of lateness this month and the effect it's having on your productivity" is a much more workable approach and is much easier for the subordinate to deal with than "I want to talk to you about your bad attitude around here."

Build on Strength.   Whenever you deal with an instance of inappropriate behavior, keep in mind that this is a unique event and that the person is highly appropriate and productive 95 percent or more of the time. Letting her know early in the conversation that you are aware of this and appreciate it will go a long way toward decreasing her defensiveness and getting her support for the behavior change that you want. Instead of saying something humiliating, consider saying something like "I'd like you to apply the same fine attention you give to detail on the job to adherence to the safety regulations."

Try to catch the person doing something *right*. This is a good habit to get into anyway, and it is especially useful in dealing with people in the process of attempting to correct inappropriate behaviors. I believe people usually get what they want. If you take appropriate behavior for granted and you call attention to inappropriate behavior, it shouldn't be much of a surprise if you end up getting what you are calling attention to. On the other hand, if you call attention to appropriate and productive behaviors and you deal with inappropriate and unproductive behaviors in a matter-of-fact way, they will probably start to improve.

Think about the respective effects of these two statements:

> "Tony, I won't have you yelling at your employees in this plant."

> "Tony, I was surprised when you yelled at Lou this morning, particularly when I remember how patient you were with him last week when you were showing him the revised specifications."

Catch the Behavior Before It Becomes a Habit. Whenever there is a chronic state of mismanagement, that is, when an inappropriate or nonproductive behavior has been occurring for more than two months, there is almost always collusion taking place between the manager and the subordinate to keep it that way. Sometimes a manager is attempting to correct inappropriate behavior but is doing it very slowly. The reason may be that she is benefiting, consciously or unconsciously, from the subordinate's inappropriate behavior or from not dealing with it.

For example, dealing with Charlie's abrasiveness would eat up a certain part of your working day, or really teaching Sara the intricacies of her job would leave you having to fill the time you regularly use to go over her work, or if you confront Fred again about being late, you'll be subjected to 20 minutes of lame excuses and whining. If the situation is a chronic one, before you actually deal with the offender, you need to take the time to get in touch with why you haven't already dealt with the situation. What might emerge from this analysis is a way to correct the inappropriate behavior that does not entail your sacrificing the benefits that you are now getting by allowing the behavior to continue.

In most cases, however, the reasons that the manager hasn't called attention to the inappropriate behavior are those that were mentioned earlier—not wanting to appear petty, not wanting to offend the person, or hoping that it will not occur again. What you as the manager need to understand is that every time you ignore an inappropriate behavior, there is collusion. In effect, your nonresponse is a clear, although quiet, message that it is okay for the surbordinate to continue doing this. Actually, you do the surbordinate an extreme disservice by not calling attention to the infraction the first time that it occurs, in that you are allowing the subordinate to get away with something now that will have to be dealt with much more harshly later on. And you do yourself a tremendous disservice as well. Once you intentionally bypass the first opportunity to correct the problem, you set a precedent. Each time that you ignore the issue, the precedent becomes more forceful and you are actually engaging in self-disempowerment. For instance, how strong is your case, and how would you respond to the following confrontation from a subordinate: "You knew that I was late three times in the last three weeks. How come you didn't say something the first time?"

Observe the Behavior Yourself. Although the contactful approach to dealing with inappropriate behavior is fairly easy, it can be made unnecessarily complicated. The last thing you want to tell a subordinate is, "I have been told by several of your co-workers that on three occasions this month you left early." The moment that you use hearsay evidence you open up a much more destructive issue. In all probability, the subordinate will now be much more concerned about who's been snitching than about leaving work a little early a few times.

When you get hearsay evidence it best to use it as an alert and then to observe the behavior yourself. Keep in mind that you can't always be certain why the information is coming to you in the first place. The person reporting the infraction may be genuinely concerned because of the effects of the inappropriate behavior on the work setting, or he may have an ulterior motive, and you could be being set up. If it is absolutely impossible to observe the behavior, at least level with the subordinate about it. Tell her what you heard and ask if it's true before going any further. If the subordinate answers yes, you can proceed to deal with the issue. If the reply is no and there is no way to check it out, I suggest that you drop the issue then and there. Maybe she didn't do it. And if she did, she now knows that she was caught and she probably won't do it again. That's not such a bad outcome!

Permanent Change Comes with Ownership

In many cases, a subordinate will give a quick promise to change a behavior in order to get out of the painful situation or to avoid future retribution. Although this will minimally fill the bill, you as a manager or parent are settling for very little, and chances are that the inappropriate behavior will occur again. In my view, the only changes that are worthwhile in an organization or a family are permanent ones. And the only way to effect a permanent change is for the individual to decide that he or she *chooses* to make the change.

In the contactful approach, you make the most impact by working with the individual in such ways that he can see that there are personal benefits to be gained from working with you and making the change in behavior. This can be accomplished only if he is willing to listen to you, and the best way I know to get that to happen is for you to listen to him first. Once he knows that you are willing to hear his side of the story and is sure that you are not there to cause injury, you will find it a lot easier to get him to hear you and even to get the cooperation that you are looking for.

The Strategy

As I mentioned before, if the inappropriate behavior is simply a result of lack of awareness or a bad judgment, a simple reminder is all that is required. However, if the situation warrants your dealing directly with the individual, there is an effective strategy that is based on the positive approach to resistance.

1. *Contactfully indicate the specific inappropriate behavior.* In this opening step, the important thing is to put the person at ease as quickly as possible. Tell him clearly what the purpose of the meeting is as soon as you can, and take care to build on his strengths whenever there is an authentic opportunity to do this. Be specific when you state the inappropriate behavior, and be prepared for him to initially show some defensiveness, hostility, or embarrassment. How *you* choose to start this meeting will be the controlling factor in whether it will be judicial or contactful.

2. *Point out the effects of the behavior and indicate that a change is needed.* Although letting the individual know about your displeasure about the occurrence is important, it is even more useful to show him the potential or actual effects of such behavior. In this way, the issue becomes depersonalized and both you and the offender can start to focus your energy on the problem rather than on the offender. The more that he can see objectively that the behavior causes a problem for the work group, himself, or the organization or family, the more willing he will be to consider changing it. Avoid the temptation to lecture or to cast desired outcomes in veiled threats. Remember that this is a problem-solving discussion!

3. *Ask for reasons for the behavior and* listen *to them.* How you conduct this step will be the biggest factor in determining whether the individual will want to work with you or against you. No matter how skillfully you conduct the meeting, he is bound to feel some defensiveness. He may feel he had good reasons for doing what he did and that his behavior was justified. It is in this step that the resistance will surface. It is vital that you surface and honor this as much as possible.

4. *Agree on a mutual action plan.* In many cases, you will have inadvertently colluded with the individual in setting the conditions for the inappropriate behavior to occur, for example, lack of recognition or boring work. Remember that it is *you* who have a problem with the behavior and who want the change. This suggests that you have a better chance of getting the change if you are willing to do something to help the person with what may be bothering or blocking him. Most important, if you know the reasons for the behavior and have responded in a contactful manner, you will have additional information about what caused the inappropriate behavior and will be in a better position to do something about it. In most cases, this step will be characterized by the individual's stating what he is willing or not willing to do and by your doing the same. It is here that you both are exploring ways to permanently rectify the situation, in terms of precipitating causes and specific behaviors and outcomes. If successful, you will come up with an option that will get you the specific behavior change that you want, and the individual will emerge with something that will be of more value than the dubious benefits that he was deriving from being inappropriate.

5. *Get a free commitment to change.* Once the agreements are made, it is necessary that the individual state clearly that the inappropriate behavior will not occur again. If he says, "I'll try," thank him for the good intention but do not settle for that. Get him to commit to what he will *do.* Do not force a commitment! If, after a good interchange, he is unwilling to make the behavior change that you require, have him state clearly first what the costs and risks are of changing the behavior and then what the costs or risks are of not changing the behavior. Once the two separate lists are in the open, ask him to choose which set of costs he prefers. In most cases, helping the offender to be this clear about potential outcomes for compliance and noncompliance, as he sees it, will be enough to get you a freely given commitment. Remember that since the offender is the one who is generating the lists of bad outcomes, you have threatened no one. If after doing this, he is still not willing to make the required behavior change, I think that you're still in

pretty good shape. What you have accomplished, at the minimum, is that you have gotten the person to take *full* responsibility for his own actions. That's not such a bad outcome either!

6. *Thank the person for cooperating.* Thanking the person for his help, as a last step, is one way to ensure that the meeting ends as a problem-solving discussion. The thing to keep in mind is that initially the inappropriate behavior was a problem for you, not for the person who committed it. By ending the meeting as you would any problem-solving meeting, you are increasing the likelihood that the individual will leave thinking of himself as a resource to the organization, not as a screw-up or a source of embarrassment.

Summary A few elements of this approach need to be highlighted. First, keep in mind that almost all people prefer to be appropriate, rather than inappropriate, all things being equal. When an intentional inappropriate behavior occurs and is then repeated, it's usually because all things are not equal in this instance. Try to find out what is wrong before coming down on the individual.

Conduct the meeting in terms of what is occurring between you and the individual, not in accordance with the step-by-step strategy just outlined. The strategy is intended as a guide for planning the meeting. If all six steps have been touched on at some point, chances are that you did it just right. Good contact is what will get you the results that you are looking for. It is achieved by staying focused on what's occurring right here, right now, between you and the other person, not on where some third party (me) might be.

Some degree of hostility, defensiveness, or embarrassment is part and parcel of this type of meeting. It's natural, so don't be put off by it. Remember that when a person is defensive or even somewhat hostile to a higher-up, the defensiveness or hostility is protective, not aggressive. The individual is protecting herself in a threatening situation. Not only could you bring about some bad outcome for her as a result of this meeting, but also she is no doubt experiencing some loss of self-esteem. The defensiveness is aimed at stopping you from hurting her, not at hurting you. You don't have to respond to the defensiveness or hostility aggressively, since you are not being attacked.

Work *with* the individual's resistance. It's healthy! By showing respect for her viewpoint, you better your work relationship and you get additional information that will be of help to you in resolving the problem.

In the absence of specific data, assume no ill intent on the part of the individual. Even if you suspect ill intent, if you deal with the person as if there were none, you increase the probability that the ill intent will diminish simply through lack of attention. Ill intent is an attitude. It's the behavior that you want changed.

Finally, remember that the key to developing a solid, productive work or interpersonal relationship lies in assisting the other person to take *full* responsibility for her actions.

CHAPTER 8

Power and Constructive Conflict

Power, as described earlier, is strictly an intrapersonal phenomenon and is measured in terms of obtained objectives. At times, however, your pursuit of an objective will run counter to another person's pursuit, and conflict will result.

Conflict can be defined as "the act of two or more individuals or groups attempting to occupy the same place at the same time." The term *space* can refer to physical space, as in wars over territory, to psychological space, as in a heated debate over principles, or to emotional space, as in two people competing for the affections of the same person. Conflict, like power, is seen by many as a negative condition, sometimes a little frightening and almost always to be avoided. In most cases, conflict is simply misunderstood. As with power, conflict has several elements.

In the first place, conflict is absolutely unavoidable. Much has been said about the uniqueness of each individual, the conclusion being that each person is much more different from than similar to anyone else. With this being the situation, it seems apparent that any long-term relationship will experience conflict at times.

Second, like power, conflict is neither good nor bad, it simply *is*. If managed poorly, it can have a negative, if not disastrous, effect on personal relationships and organizational effectiveness. If managed effectively, it can have very positive outcomes.

Third, conflict provides two elements that are essential to the survival and growth of any organization. Conflict is the organization's prime source of energy. And when managed well, it is also the organization's prime source of creativity. Conflict is to organizations what gasoline is to an internal combustion engine. It does have a potential for volatility and destructiveness if mishandled. But if respected and understood, it keeps the system running. For example, I have never seen anyone, myself included, who enters a conflict situation without being alert, active, and ready to engage other people openly.

Also, when a system is staffed by individuals who are powerful and who are clear about what they want, there is a much higher probability that more unique and creative alternatives will emerge in the attempt to provide the most people with what they want in any given situation. When you view conflict as a potentially positive force in organizations, the strategy becomes one of utilizing conflict, rather than constantly searching for ways to resolve it. It is the *issue* that requires resolution, not the conflict per se.

Fourth, conflict occurs mostly among individuals who are personally or organizationally interdependent. Although this may not be so in some settings (for example, political or international arenas), it is almost always the case within the family or the working system. Were there not a mutual need at issue among the conflicting parties, there would be no need for the parties to engage. That is, if I did not need your support or contribution to achieve my ends, or if I didn't need the resource that you have, I would simply go elsewhere for what I want and not hassle with you.

Fifth, there is much *less* damage caused to people and organizations by conflict than by avoiding conflict. Conflict, when expressed openly and contactfully, will sometimes be uncomfortable or even painful but will not create permanent damage or leave scar tissue. Conflict that is intentionally avoided or suppressed very quickly turns to resentment and hatred, particularly if one or both parties are angry. This is where the real damage occurs.

Locus of Conflict

Conflict in the organizational setting will usually be over fact, method, objective, or value. Conflict over *fact* is the most objective type of conflict and is therefore the easiest to resolve. Conflict over fact usually involves what a thing is, and it can be dealt with by mutually agreeing on a criterion or a reference to make a final decision.

For example:

C: It's a buffalo.
P: It's a duck.

C: It's a BUFFALO!!

P: It's a DUCK, DAMMIT!!!

This one is easy to resolve. You kick the thing. If it says "Mooo," it's a buffalo; if it says "Quack," it's a duck. End of conflict. Or if you don't like that approach you can always use the corporate solution. Hire a consultant and he'll tell you what it is.

Conflict over *method* is still predominantly objective, but it begins to incorporate some subjective judgment and personal opinion. Conflict over method usually deals with what is to be done. Although it has somewhat more potential for volatility than conflict over fact, it can be dealt with by discussing the pros and cons in terms of environmental conditions. For example, a conflict over how to conduct a sales campaign can be resolved easily by getting mutual agreement on market conditions, advertising capabilities, budget constraints, and so forth.

Conflict over *objectives* is more subjective than objective and has more potential for volatility than the first two types. Conflict over objectives usually deals with what is to be accomplished. This type of conflict will be harder fought because it involves personal commitments and risks. Conflict over objectives, although often involving organizational variables, such as what is best for the company, also involves the personal objectives of those involved in the conflict, for example, getting the next promotion. The basic strategy for engaging in this type of conflict is to recognize the legitimacy of the subjective elements and of the objective ones as well. Once this legitimacy is established, the tactic is to deal with them accordingly. Recognize that each individual has a legitimate right to his subjective or personal concerns, and work with the objective elements in terms of what is available within the environment. Knowing each person's subjective concerns will guide you in finding a solution that will be accepted.

Conflict over *values* is almost totally subjective and therefore has the most potential for volatility. Conflict over values deals with what is right and wrong. Mismanaged conflicts over values frequently result in divorces, at one extreme, and holy wars, at the other. The basic strategy in dealing with this kind of conflict is to avoid it if at all possible. If it is unavoidable, then the approach is to objectify the issue as much as possible, that is, to deal with *behaviors* or *events* that arise from the value and not to deal with the value itself. For example, a heated argument over the moral rightness of capital punishment has a high probability of ending in nothing but rage and righteous and moral indignation. A discussion of capital punishment in terms of its deterrent effects and its legal ramifications has somewhat better chances of resulting in agreement and resolution.

Myths About Conflict

The principal reason why so many people fear and want to avoid conflict is that they are responding to the myriad myths that surround it. Even when people engage in conflict and the resuts are disastrous, it is because what they did was based on the myth of conflict, not on the reality of conflict. The first step, therefore, in becoming more comfortable and effective in the conflict situation is to demystify the subject. Here are some of the more commonly held misconceptions about conflict.

We're all gonna die! The myth here is that if we engage in an open conflict, the ultimate result is that I will end up dead or some variation of "dead," such as fired, disgraced, or demoted. There is much in our environment that reinforces this myth. In the movies, villains are almost always wiped out in their final conflict with the "forces of good." In real life, direct conflict sometimes results in divorces, schoolyard fights, and even the occasional firing.

However, there are two elements that people are not taking note of. The first is that nobody ever died because someone else was simply angry with him or because somebody wanted something different. This kind of unavoidable disagreement is natural and can be dealt with rationally. The second is that there are an infinite number of options for how you engage in a conflict, only one of which is the winner-take-all tactic. Unfortunately, many people see this as the only approach to conflict and its only objective, so they always approach conflict from this position. I contend very strongly that most of the outcomes of conflicts that are disastrous for one or both parties occur because the parties are locked into this viewpoint.

You won't love me! The myth here is that all good relationships are founded exclusively on trust, love, and support, and there is never any room for mistrust, anger, or disagreement. This view results in the belief that it is not possible for you to love me and be angry with me at the same time. Thus, if we are in conflict over anything, you do not love me and I am now abandoned—which is pretty scary stuff!

In all relationships, regardless of the parties' particular values, trust will coexist with mistrust, anger will coexist with love, and enlightened self-interest will coexist with support for the other person. By honoring these "negative" attributes and recognizing that they are just as natural and protective as the "positive" ones, you have a more secure position on which to base conflict situations. The best example I can think of is to ask you to attend to what you are feeling the next time you have to punish or discipline your young son or daughter.

It will never stop! The myth here is that if we engage in a conflict, the conflict will go on forever. This myth is particularly virulent when there has been no open conflict for a long time or when the relationship is a relatively new one and the parties do not know each other very well yet. A variation of this myth is: If we make it okay to be in conflict over this particular issue, we will always choose conflict as a way of dealing with each other.

The fact is, of course, that everything does stop when it is finally over. The trick is to know when that is. Nobody laughs forever at the same joke, no matter how funny it was originally. Nobody cries forever over a loss, no matter how painful the loss was at the time. By recognizing that the "forever" feeling of the conflict is not the reality, you can bring forward more awareness and choices to deal with the issue realistically. After all, the longest conflict in history, the Hundred Years War, only lasted 116 years.

It's not civilized. The myth here originates in our constant desire to get as much distance as possible between ourselves and the rest of the animal kingdom. The more civilized the culture or the particular stratum within the culture, the more open conflict is held in disdain. A fight in a dockside bar might generate some amusement or even some active interest; a word spoken in anger over brandy and cigars at a formal dinner will raise eyebrows and cause consternation for months.

In fact, we may be the only species that kills for the pure fun of it. Whether it be clubbing cute little baby seals to death with a baseball bat in one hand and a beer in the other or gently riding to the hounds in formal attire to watch a bunch of dogs chew up a fox, when push comes to shove, we aren't all that civilized anyway.

Conflict is not a function of social norms, although the way it is expressed often is. Conflict, regardless of the culture, will exist any time two people try to occupy the same space at the same time. The more that people see this as a *natural state,* the higher the probability that they will deal with conflict in a truly civilized manner, that is, causing as little pain as possible in the process.

I'll lose 'em all. This particular myth probably generates more bad tactics than the others. The myth here is that the result of any particular conflict will automatically predict the outcome of all subsequent conflicts. Since each conflict is viewed as a life-or-death struggle, there is a very strong tendency to either underreact (avoid the conflict) if there is the least likelihood that the outcome will be negative or to overreact (approach the conflict with overkill) in an attempt to ensure the win at all costs.

Each and every conflict situation has a life and character of its own. Again, the need to see situations as different, rather than as similar, comes sharply into focus. The outcome of one conflict, although it certainly has some impact, is not the determiner of the outcome of the next conflict or of any other conflict.

Take the situation where you have beaten me three times in a row over the same issue. The fact that you now have three wins under your belt, rather than two, will cause some change in your perception of you. The fact that I have survived three losses and may be contemplating a fourth confrontation must also cause some change in your perception of me. We have both learned some new things about ourselves and each other in terms of how we each won or lost this one, and we have reevaluated our views about each other and the objectives accordingly. The next conflict is a brand new ball game. The main thing to keep in mind about this myth is that your expectation of a loss can become a self-fulfilling prophecy.

Low-Yield Approaches to Conflict

Although almost any approach to conflict in a given situation will have some potential for effectiveness, some strategies are more effective than others. A *strategy* is a consciously chosen approach to obtain a medium- or long-term objective. A *tactic* is a consciously chosen response to a specific situation, usually where the result is seen immediately.

There are seven approaches to conflict management. Four are used mainly to avoid it and three are used to deal with it. The four avoidance approaches are suppression, giving in, ignoring, and common-grounding. I strongly suggest that these be avoided because they offer only temporary solutions and tend to aggravate the situation rather than ameliorate it.

The three for dealing with conflict are competition, compromise, and collaboration, with compromise being the least preferred.

Suppression

Suppression is the conscious act of withholding open expression. When this strategy is used in an organization, a family, or a one-to-one relationship, the approach is to punish any act or statement that could in any way be interpreted as being hostile or aggressive. Often the punishment for such acts is far harsher than what the negative outcome of the actual conflict would have been. The end result, of course, is that there is no observable conflict.

Organizations and families that use this strategy are identifiable in several ways. Interpersonal relations are usually quite formal, for example, it's "Father" rather than "Daddy," or it's "Mr. Smith" rather than "Pete." The atmosphere is cool and calm. Most of the interaction revolves around organizational or family issues rather than interpersonal issues. Being rational is highly valued; being emotional is not. And often there is a deep concern with being, or at least appearing to be, "civilized."

Conflict is never apparent in this system, but there are high costs for keeping things this way. Because such a high value is placed on keeping things cool, calm, and collected, it is frequently difficult to locate the energy in the group. Probably the most damaging aspect is that although to the casual observer the environment is calm and conflict-free, in reality, conflict is being worked in unproductive and often damaging ways. In effect, the informal organization takes over. Rumor and gossip mills may start. Intergroup and interpersonal cooperation may appear adequate but really aren't sufficient to achieve the required results. Halfhearted support is offered and accepted. Cliques form. And there is a tendency to avoid people, rather than to contact them authentically.

The most obvious example of the harmful aspects of this approach is the approach's effects on kids. If a teacher breaks up a fight between two 6-year-olds, punishes them for fighting, and then forces them to shake hands and be friends before either is ready to do so, the result will be tattling behaviors. Both kids are still angry with each other, and the expression of this anger has been interrupted and then blocked. The anger still needs some place to go, so the kids start snitching on each other to the teacher. This expression of anger is much more destructive than the fight, since it deepens the level of the conflict. The problem is compounded by the fact that the teacher now has to reward the kids for their destructive behaviors—that is, they are both being good little boys who are helping teacher to enforce the rules. The adult counterpart of tattling is behaviors such as sniping at the other guy's project, not offering the best resource available, and damning by faint praise.

Giving In

A second low-yield way of dealing with conflict is to refuse to engage in it by totally giving in on the issue. This approach is a response to the myth that you won't love me anymore if we have a conflict. Members of organizations and families characterized by this approach usually deal with each other confluently rather than contactfully. "We'll do anything to keep peace in the family," is one way this strategy is often expressed. They may openly express warmth and support for each other, but these expressions may not be quite authentic. They place a very high value on getting along well, often to the detriment of organizational effectiveness and results. They are overly concerned with the welfare of others, and they may go to extraordinary lengths to avoid causing pain of any kind to anyone in the system. Obviously, they see conflict, or even the thought of it, as a clear threat to the group's welfare, and they avoid it at all costs.

Conflict in this situation is nonexistent, and the costs, again, are quite high. Although the group can function effectively when things are going well, a lot of energy is expended on staying unaware when things are not going well. Energy is spent in justifying other people's behaviors and in avoiding any outbreak of conflict. In using supression to deal with conflict, people tend to say, "It's all *their* fault." In giving in, people tend to say, "It's all my fault."

In using this strategy, organizational and family resources are squandered in an attempt to keep people eternally happy.

Ignoring

Some people believe that if you ignore conflict, it will go away. The slogan for this approach is: So what's the big deal? The atmosphere is casual, and relationships are generally easygoing.

When conflict is avoided, many issues, often critical ones, are ignored. There is unspoken collusion on the part of all group members to let issues slide. The result is that an energy void and, often, a creativity void slowly emerge. The effect is that people get comfortable with the increasing no-conflict state of things, so that the family or organization moves more and more in this direction with very little awareness that it is doing so.

The most damaging aspect of this strategy is that problems or issues that could have been dealt with easily and effectively when they first emerged become much more difficult and dangerous to resolve with each passing day.

Common-Grounding

This low-yield strategy is not necessarily characteristic of any particular group. Common-grounding refers to attempting to get a satisfactory resolution to a conflict as quickly as possible by finding some common ground—points of agreement or commonly shared values—among the conflicting parties.

This probably doesn't sound bad, but as a primary strategy it has several pitfalls. First, the thrust is on ending the conflict rather than on coming up with the highest-quality solution. That is, the main concern is with the fact that people are angry with each other rather than with the reason for their anger.

Second, since the aim is to end the conflict, the first solution that will end it is likely to be adapted, and needless to say, the first solution isn't necessarily the best solution. The frequent result is that only a temporary or stopgap measure is employed, leaving the participants still vulnerable and/or only partially satisfied.

Third, common-grounding is founded on the erroneous assumption that we are all essentially alike. The reality is that we are all essentially different. Attempting to resolve a heatedly contested issue by relying on a myth about human nature does not enhance the probability for a productive outcome.

It is important to note that although these low-yield approaches are generally maladaptive as strategies, they may be excellent alternatives as tactics. For example, temporarily suppressing a conflict may be highly desirable when there is an inspection team on-site. Giving in to your side in a conflict is quite appropriate when I particularly care about you and the issue is much more important to you than it is to me. Compromising on a minor point in order to obtain a major one or in order to break a deadlock is a time-honored tactic. Ignoring a minor issue or letting some things pass without comment is a very powerful tactic, since it allows you to use your time and energy as you choose. The alternative would be to fight every minor skirmish every time and accomplish little of value at the end of it all. Finally, looking for the common ground is a very positive thing to do *after* the conflict has been honored and the differences surfaced. At this stage, finding the areas where we are interdependent and actually have the same concerns is often the first step toward developing a mutually satisfying and permanent solution.

Of course, conflicts are also managed by dealing with the issues rather than evading them. As mentioned earlier, competition, compromise, and collaboration are the three possible approaches to dealing with conflict.

Competition

As a conflict strategy, competition results in a win/lose outcome. I want A but can't abide B. You want B but can't abide A. We have a direct confrontation, winner gets all, loser gets nothing. All athletic events operate on this model and it is quite appropriate to organizations that are competing for a share of the market. It is also appropriate within organizations under certain circumstances, such as when you and I are competing for the same promotion.

Compromise

Compromise is probably the most popular and least effective means of approaching conflict. In fact, it is often looked upon not only as an approach to dealing with conflict, but as a virtue in itself. "You have to learn to compromise" is the constant cry of the powerless to the powerful. When competition is cast in terms of win/lose, compromise results in a lose/lose outcome. That is, I want A and can't abide B, and you want B and can't abide A. I agree to diminish a part of A if you agree to diminish a part of B. You agree, and then come back with a counteroffer for more of the same. We stay at it until we are both sure that neither of us will end up with anything that we don't want. The problem here is that we don't end up getting much of what we do want either. By focusing almost exclusively on what we each don't want rather than on what we each do want, chances are that no one will get much of anything. Consider the difference between a legislative bill in its original draft and what it looks like when it finally becomes a law. Or, in more personal terms: you want to go to the mountains, your spouse wants to go to the shore, so you compromise and end up spending two weeks in Cleveland.

Organizations that accept compromise as the norm for dealing with conflict have several characteristics: They can meet standards but do not excel. The roles and expectations of various group members are frequently blurred and misunderstood. Disparate values are rarely discussed and hardly ever come to the surface. There seems to be a lot of organizational activity, but none of its outcome is of high quality. If the organization could be described in a single word, it would be *mediocre*.

Collaboration

Collaboration is thought of as a win/win strategy. In collaboration, I want A but not B and you want B but not A. We agree from the start that we will stay with the conflict, no matter how long it takes, until we come up with C. C is the unique solution that will provide both of us with all of what we want out of the situation. Note that collaboration is the only one of the three strategies dealing with conflict that emphasizes the generation of a third alternative. Do not confuse collaboration with compromise! In collaboration nothing of value is given up to resolve the conflict or to reach agreement.

All things being equal (though they rarely are) the collaborative approach is the best of the three. Second best is competition, since it does result in some positive gain with reasonable risk, if it is handled effectively. The least desirable is compromise. Compromise should be reserved for situations in which neither of the other approaches will work, such as when you and the other person are of equal strength, the issue is not a critical one, and you have run out of time.

Conditions for Constructive Conflict

Constructive conflict is a term that refers more to the outcome of the conflict than to the actual process that the conflict entails. A constructive conflict is one in which (1) the outcome or solution is acceptable to both parties, (2) no party to the conflict was unnecessarily injured, (3) the relationships are at the least no worse off than before the conflict emerged, and (4) the family or organization will somehow benefit or be in better shape as a result of the conflict.

When you consciously choose to engage an individual or a group in a conflict situation, several conditions should exist in order to ensure the greatest likelihood of a positive outcome. In fact, I suggest putting off any direct confrontation or engagement until both sides are confident that these conditions exist.

Willingness to Engage

Both sides must be willing to confront the issue openly. If one party is anxious to engage but the other is not, there is little likelihood that anything positive will emerge. That is, if you want to talk to me but I don't want to talk to you, that's it for right now. Any attempt to cajole or threaten me into engaging with you will result in my being even less willing to do so. A unilateral surprise attack will have the same or probably even a more disastrous effect. Your best approach is to find out why I don't want to talk to you and, if possible, deal with that. If that information isn't available, the best thing to do is to back off and just leave the situation where it is for the time being.

Relatively Equal Strength

At the outset, it is important that the two parties see each other as being equally strong. This view can come in many forms. We could be relatively equal on the same dimension, such as physical size or organizational position. Or we could be relatively equal on different dimensions: I may be stronger, but you may be faster. Or you may represent a large, influential organization and be able to bring much pressure to bear, but I may be able to offset some of your influence with my greater flexibility. Or you may be more determined to win than I am, but I may have less to lose and so be willing to risk a little more.

It matters not how parity is determined, only that it exist. Without this, there is little chance for a productive outcome. If I am actually weaker than you or simply see myself as weaker, I will be afraid to engage you for fear of getting hurt. If you are weaker or I see you as weaker, I may treat you with kid gloves for fear of damaging you.

Keep in mind that the object of constructive conflict is not to destroy the other party; in almost all cases, you are interdependent and may need each other's support later on. The object is to emerge with a satisfactory solution without destroying the working or supportive relationship.

Several years ago I was involved in a team-building effort with a city executive staff. At one point during a meeting break, a mid-level manager openly disagreed with a point that the city manager had made. The city manager swung on his subordinate with what can only be described as blind rage. Apparently these two men had a history of strained relations and this was the straw that broke the camel's back. The subordinate manager was devastated and the city manager was just getting his second wind. I immediately suggested that the three of us go to another room and attempt to get this straightened out.

In this situation, the city manager was clearly the stronger of the two. Not only was he the chief executive and two levels above the subordinate, he was bigger, stronger, older, and better educated. What I suggested, with both parties agreeing, was that I, as the consultant, would ally myself with the subordinate manager. In effect, it would be both of us against "the boss." The aim was to clear the situation, and one of the conditions was that the subordinate manager was still so upset that he had difficulty speaking.

My initial function was as "alter ego" for the subordinate manager. That is, it was agreed that I would speak for him and if I did not represent his views or concerns accurately, he would interrupt me and tell me. After this went on for about 15 minutes, the subordinate manager realized that the city manager was coming across straight and strong in what he had to say, and nobody was getting hurt in the interchange. At this point, he began to speak for himself, and my role switched to that of interpreter. I maintained a neutral position and monitored the conversation, making sure that each party was clear about what the other was saying. After about 20 minutes of this, they decided to go out and continue the dialogue over dinner and I was free to go back to the bar.

No Sandbagging

Sandbagging is the tactic of keeping one weapon hidden from your opponent. When your opponent is temporarily distracted or off his guard, you whip out the sandbag and clobber him with it.

An element that is essential to the successful handling of conflict is that both parties agree, ahead of time, that all the weapons will be out on the table. In most cases where the conditions are being set for a conflict, it is unrealistic for you and your opponent to talk in terms of trust. What is really required here is that you attend to the areas of *mistrust*. Before there is any expression of conflict, the mistrust must be sufficiently reduced to allow both of you to engage in the conflict with a reasonable degree of safety. Obviously, if neither of you is willing to accept the assurances of the other, or if you cannot get assurances from the other that are acceptable to you, it would be a mistake to for you to engage in the conflict at this point.

Several ways to decrease mistrust prior to engaging in a conflict are for the parties to:

1. Specify what areas are to be discussed and what issues, if any, will not be touched on except by mutual consent.
2. Agree ahead of time that either party can disengage at any time.
3. Agree on who should attend the discussions and who should not.
4. State expectations for the discussions in realistic terms. For example, "For right now we would simply like to hear what you have to say," or "We have no expectation of coming to a resolution at this early stage."

In their early stages, most conflicts are characterized by varying degrees of mistrust on both sides. Usually some of this mistrust is appropriate, and some of it is not. In approaching the issue in the way described here, you surface and eliminate those areas of mutual mistrust that are based on myth, faulty expectations, or misinformation. Then you can address and work through the areas of real mistrust as you get to know each other in subsequent meetings.

Keep in mind that when the conflict issue is deepseated and personally important to both of you, or when you don't have a history of a good relationship, the objective of the early meetings is simply for the two of you to be together in the same room with neither of you getting hurt.

Clear Objectives

Being clear about what you want is an essential element in any issue concerning power. And nowhere is it more important than in the area of conflict. Conflicts often escalate and relations get unnecessarily damaged simply because one or both parties were not crystal clear about what they wanted.

The biggest problem here is that if you and your opponent are not clear about what you want, you will be equally unsure about when the conflict should be over. The second biggest problem is that the less clear both of you are, the higher the probability that you will be distracted by side issues or personal remarks. So first, sit down and get as clear as possible on what you want, what you are willing to settle for if a fall-back position becomes necessary, and what would clearly be unacceptable to you.

Commitment to a Collaborative Solution

As mentioned earlier, there are three major approaches to conflict in families and organizations: collaboration, competition, and compromise, in descending order of desirability. Both of you must consciously agree ahead of time that you are opting for the collaborative approach. This means that both of you will adhere to the following conditions for the duration of the conflict or until you mutually agree to change the approach.

1. Either of you is free to say as much or as little as you choose.
2. Neither of you will be expected to agree to anything that you are not honestly in agreement with and honestly willing to support.
3. Both of you are willing to stay engaged over this matter for as long as time permits and conditions require.
4. You are both clearly committed to the premise that a mutually acceptable solution is available.

5. In conditions of stress or time pressures, it may be advisable for both of you to agree to a fall-back position ahead of time, such as "If we can't come to an honest accord in three weeks, it's every man for himself."

Common Language

A small but important point to check out before you initiate any constructive conflict is whether you both speak the same language. It is essential that all parties enter the situation with the ability to at least partially understand everybody's position. *Common language* refers either to the condition where both of you share a common set of values, background, and jargon, or to the condition where both of you are aware and tolerant of each other's values, reference points, and means of personal expression.

There are myriad examples of the need for common language among conflicting parties. In my opinion, the student riots of the 1960s were greatly escalated because neither the students nor the university administrators had the capability or the desire to understand the other side. Most screaming arguments between parents and children have the same affliction.

A particularly dramatic work-related example occurred several years ago in a drug abuse agency that I was working with. The managerial team consisted of 14 people, most of whom had widely differing backgrounds. At the time, the group members were barely getting along well enough to work together. The week before, a physical scuffle had broken out at the agency between two of the managers.

Mark, one of the combatants, was extremely resistant to dealing with feelings. As a matter of fact, he had approached me before the two-day session and had warned me in no uncertain terms that he would absolutely not deal with feelings during the session. He was willing to discuss anything logically and to deal with facts, but that was it! The other combatant, Greg, was very excitable. Occasionally, his feelings would come so quickly and intensely that he had difficulty expressing them.

Physical violence is a universally unacceptable way of dealing with conflict in organizations, yet because of their widely disparate values and backgrounds, these two men seemed to have no other way available at the time to fully express their deep and real differences about the issue at hand.

As was to be expected, it wasn't long into the first day before the unfinished argument between Mark and Greg erupted. In dealing with this, I took on the role of temporary interpreter. Greg would let out a blast of anger, whereupon I would turn to Mark and say, "The point that Greg is attemping to convey is. . . ." Mark would respond with an intellectual interpretation of the event, and I would say to Greg, "Mark is really steamed because. . . ." We managed to get some closure on the issue, and by the end of the day, Mark and Greg had begun to communicate with each other directly.

In summary, if conflict is seen as a source of potential devastation rather than as a specific means to a specific end, it could become very frightening, indeed. If what each of us wants were never desired by anyone else, there would never be conflict, but this is hardly what life is like in vital families and organizations.

To begin to get more comfortable with conflict, it is essential that you see that being comfortable with conflict is a necessary part of being powerful. Next, realize that conflict does not necessarily imply injury, ruptured relationships, or organizations in ruins. Finally, and most importantly, be aware that as you become more comfortable and knowledgeable about conflict, you will increase your control of each conflict that you engage in. You have the choice of being either a manager or a victim of conflict.

CHAPTER 9

The Art of Creative Fighting

A common reason that many people are unwilling to engage others powerfully is that they simply lack awareness of the basic rules for effective fighting. According to a popularly held view, people need to know how to get along well during a fight. On the other hand, I think that the time to know how to get along well is after the fight is over. What people need to know during a fight is how to fight well. Many a young child will allow himself to be intimidated by other kids until his Dad gives him a few basic lessons in the art of self-defense. The paradox, of course, is that once the child is comfortable with his newly acquired skills, there is much less likelihood of his having to use them. The newly acquired knowledge produces a clear confidence that is observable to others, which makes him less subject to attacks. On the other hand, if a fight does become unavoidable, he can handle it.

Anger is as appropriate and productive a reaction to events as is any other human response. Anger is the natural reaction to frustration and is as unavoidably reflexive a reaction to being blocked as laughter is to being amused. If I, by accident or design, have done something to frustrate a plan of yours, or have blocked your progress toward a goal, you have every right to feel anger toward me. As a matter of fact, at least as an initial reaction, it is the most appropriate response.

Whether it is appropriate to feel anger is not the issue; rather, the issue is how we can deal with anger appropriately when it does occur. By acknowledging the legitimacy of conflict and establishing the norms for fighting, we introduce little threat to the ongoing relationship.

Fighting Is Natural and Appropriate

People need to see fighting as a natural and at times very appropriate thing to do. It's even fun occasionally, so long as both parties agree to do it. Above all, don't view fighting as an activity to be avoided at all costs. Whenever two or more people are working or living together, there will be conflicts of interest. Sometimes these can be resolved by peaceful negotiation or willing compliance—and sometimes they cannot! When they cannot, fighting is the ultimate and appropriate response, unless one party disempowers himself and gives in out of fear of engaging the other.

Fighting, when engaged in creatively, has several positive aspects: It is energizing. It honors both parties. It frequently produces the best solution under the circumstances. It strengthens, rather than weakens, the relationship.

When fighting is not engaged in creatively, it has many negative aspects and usually a negative outcome; and the end result is that fighting becomes something to be avoided even more. Work and personal relationships become characterized by spitefulness, sniping, silent vows to get revenge, sulking, self-pity, and the eternal whine "No one understands me."

Deal with One Issue at a Time

More often than not in an ongoing relationship, unfinished business coexists with the current cause of contention. The temptation when fighting is to get in a "shot" whenever and however you can. Frequently, this is done by suddenly resurfacing a past, unresolved argument and catching your opponent offguard. This may begin: "Oh, yeah? Well, what about the time that you. . . ?" If you are successful with this ploy, you gain the upper hand and your opponent is clearly put on the defensive. The problem is that you are now fighting a different fight that has no relevance to the current conflict. And this not only disempowers you in connection with the current issue, but also makes you vulnerable to a similar shot in an area in which you are unguarded.

The tactic here is to keep all your energy focused on the *current* point of contention. If your opponent suddenly surfaces a second, unrelated issue, respond with something like "All right, but that's *not* what we're dealing with at the moment." It's okay to bracket the second issue and set it aside for future consideration; above all, don't attempt to deal with it now.

The exception to this is the situation in which a current fight surfaces an unfinished issue that is actually blocking resolution on the current point of contention—for example, "The last time you asked me for support and I helped you, you refused to acknowledge my contribution in the final report." If this is the case, bracket the current issue cleanly, and attempt to get closure on the unfinished piece that is blocking the contact between you. Once that issue is successfully resolved, you can return to the current fight with more energy and greater chances for a successful outcome. Regardless of which issue you consciously choose to address, it's still *one* issue at a time.

Pick Your Arena

Just because someone is angry with you and wants to engage you on an issue does not automatically mean that you have to engage her. Too often you may be dragged into the combat zone unready or uninterested. This can result in your feeling unfairly ambushed and can create even more defensiveness, resentment, resistance, and animosity. The counter for this is to be aware that it takes two people to fight and if you don't happen to want to fight right now, there just won't be a fight right now.

There are three basic approaches to consider when a fight is looming on the horizon, all of which can be appropriate.

1. *Engage.* If the timing is right and the point is legitimate, the sooner the problem is surfaced and dealt with creatively, the better. The longer a fight stays internalized, the higher the probability that the hostility will increase and that the conflict, when it becomes overt, will be more interpersonally volatile.

2. *Let it go.* If the issue is important to the other party but not important to you, sometimes it is okay to simply let the other person have it. Before engaging in a fight, you have to assess whether the particular issue is worth your time and effort. If it isn't, it makes little sense to put your time and energy into pursuing a goal that doesn't matter much to you. Also, by *letting it go* when appropriate, you have turned an opponent into an ally. He now owes you one. Remember, if you *consciously choose* to accede to the other's wishes, you have lost no power.

3. *Put it on hold.* If you are engaged before you are ready, you have the option of acknowledging the issue and bracketing it. That is, listen to what the other person is saying; acknowledge that you understand the point being made and the importance of it to her; and then *set a time* for getting back together and dealing with it. This tends to defuse the issue for the other person and will, at least, stop it from escalating any further. This also will give you the time that you need to consider the issue fully and to get your "ducks lined up."

Also, remember that this strategy goes both ways. That is, avoid forcing an opponent into a confrontation with you before she is willing to engage you. By adopting this strategy, you avoid the risk of an overreation or an unwarranted or unexpected counterattack.

Get It Out the First Time, Get It Right the Second Time

In the heat of battle, things are often said that are regretted an instant later, particularly when the issue is of deep personal significance to one or both parties, when there is a high degree of ego involvement, or when the relationship is an important one. Also, whether you are angry or not, you may not always know exactly what you feel or think until you actually hear yourself say it.

An important element of creative fighting is to create enough room to allow the unexpected or the unintentional statement to surface without escalating the fight. When the unexpected or unwarranted statement occurs, stop the action and check out whether that is, in fact, what the other party *really* meant to convey. If your opponent disavows it, let it drop right there! If he confirms it, a real and deeper point of contention may have surfaced, and now you both have a choice as to which element to work on. Of course, give yourself the same latitude in backing away from statements that you don't mean.

Avoid an Early Resolution

One of the most mindless pieces of advice that is universally offered to newly married couples is: "Never let the sun set on an argument." A fight will be over when it is time for it to be over. You can certainly make a fight last longer than it should, but you can practically never make a fight end before it should. When you resolve a fight too quickly, or you rush into a simple, but incomplete, resolution, several negative side effects occur that are usually more painful and damaging in the long run than the original fight itself.

First, certain elements of the fight may be left unfinished. These do not go away; they are temporarily repressed, only to surface later on. Secondly, the easiest solution is not always the best one, in that it tends to cover up the real issue; in other words, you risk treating the symptom rather than the problem. Third, if the resolution is complete for you but not for me, I am likely to deal with you in other areas, such as intimacy or trust, with a little less enthusiasm than if the issue were completely resolved for me. This side effect, although very subtle, can be very damaging to the relationship.

Each fight has a different level of intensity. Some fights involve simple disagreements and are resolvable by "sundown." Others involve intense feelings, deepseated values, or complex issues, and it takes much more time to deal with them effectively. It is essential to consider the time element an important component of what's going on right now.

There are two basic tactics that you can use to ensure that the proper time element is not lost when you engage in a creative fight. The first is that both you and your opponent should clearly and specifically recognize the complexity and importance of the issue to both of you, and then you should mutually agree to give the issue all the time that it needs.

The second tactic, *bracketing*, is also quite useful, particularly if the relationship is an involved and interdependent one and the issue is complex. Many times reality dictates that life or work must go on, even though you are currently involved in a fight. When this is the case, it's okay to fight and then bracket the fight cleanly and put your combined energies into other, more salient issues. As long as the fight is bracketed, you can get back to it as soon as the situation allows. In many instances, this will allow you and your opponent to work together well and energetically in other areas not affected by the fight. This is possible because the point of contention, although "on hold," is still actively being honored by both of you.

Don't Call Names

The whole function of creative fighting is to manage a conflict in such a way that (1) an effective resolution can be found, (2) both parties can maintain a clear sense of personal dignity throughout, and (3) the relationship is not damaged. I can think of nothing that will more negatively affect these objectives than resorting to name calling.

The objective of creative fighting is to get what you want, as opposed to the "garden variety," or street variety, of fighting, where the objective is to inflict as much injury on the opponent as possible. In most cases, these two objectives are mutually exclusive, so that you have to make a clear choice as to which one you want. If what you are after is to get what you want, then making every effort not to dehumanize your opponent is very much in your best interest.

People usually resort to name calling when logical arguments fail or when their tolerance for frustration has been exceeded. Suppose that you don't believe the information that your opponent is imparting to you. Stating firmly, "I don't believe the information that you just gave me," which, granted, is somewhat provocative, would be far better than turning on your opponent and shouting, "You're a damned bloody liar!"

Name calling can range from using descriptive epithets to making *any* statement that implies anything at all about the personality of your opponent. In any creative fight, it is safest and most productive to speak only for yourself. If you speak only in terms of what you want, what you are experiencing, or what you are thinking, you run very little risk of personally offending your opponent and thereby escalating the fight to a more volatile and unmanageable level.

If I state that I don't believe something that you just said, I am speaking strictly about my belief; I am not calling you a liar. By focusing only on what I am experiencing, I am allowing you the option to question why I don't believe what you just said. If you countered my statement of disbelief with "Are you calling me a liar?" I would respond, "Certainly not. I am merely saying that I don't believe the information, and here's why. . . ."

Don't Corner Your Opponent

At one time or another we have all probably reveled in that most delightful of fantasies, the one where we have our archenemy on his knees, begging and pleading for mercy. As a fantasy, it's terrific; as an objective, it's rarely, if ever, productive.

There is no doubt that on occasion being "right" and devastating your opponent are more personally satisfying than is getting the best resolution available in terms of outcomes. The problem with this momentary satisfaction is just that—the satisfaction is only momentary, and it has high costs associated with it. First, by cornering and devastating your opponent, you may have sacrificed the solid resolution that would have been available had you been willing to fight a little longer. Second, although you have crippled your opponent, you haven't killed him. Sooner or later he is going to be back in action, and you can bet that either he will actively stalk you or he will lay a trap for you, ready to be sprung at the first opportunity.

The longer a fight goes on, regardless of the point of contention, the greater the ego involvement on both sides of the argument. That is, as the length of the fight increases, so does the need to save face. The strategy is to do everything in your power to make it as easy as you can for your opponent to give you what you want. Go out of your way, if necessary, to allow your opponent to save face. Sometimes this may even entail helping your opponent to avoid a trap that you see coming that he may not—for example, not responding to an ultimatum that he has just delivered to you.

This face-saving tactic can be particularly productive for you if both you and your opponent can see clearly that he is going to lose this one. By allowing your opponent to retire gracefully from the field, you may not only have gotten what you wanted but also have accorded the "enemy" the respect that he deserves. This stance on your part usually results in some degree of appreciation on the part of the vanquished opponent, particularly when you both know that you could have inflicted a lot more pain and humiliation if you had chosen to do so.

Agree to Disagree

Creative fighting, like any other expression of power, demands the generation of alternatives and conscious choice. Although a mutually acceptable resolution is always the desired outcome, on some issues this may not be available. In fights where the point of contention is basically objective, as in arguing over a fact or a method, mutually acceptable resolutions are almost always available. But in fights over deeper, more personal issues, such as objectives or values, mutuality is much more difficult and sometimes impossible to achieve.

In arguments of a deeply personal nature, such as over religion, the value is such an innate part of the individual that she will experience any attack on the value or its validity as a personal attack on her. In such a case, it will be almost impossible for her to concede a point without feeling personally diminished in the process.

The best and most obvious choice in dealing with arguments of this type is to avoid them if at all possible. Sometimes, however, you and another person will engage in a discussion over one point, only to discover that a deeper, more intense point is really what is at issue. Take a husband and wife discussing the upcoming divorce of mutual friends:

W: Isn't it awful about the Joneses getting divorced?

H: What's so awful? They never got along.

W: Yes, but they owe it to each other to try to work it out.

H: I think that ten years constitutes a damn good try.

W: Well, I think that too many couples are taking the easy way out. Divorce is just too easy and too acceptable a solution today.

H: Well, I think that people are wise to end things when they're over. Too many people stay together when they would be better off apart.

One choice here is for each party to continue to badger the other to see it his or her way. Although this can be a tempting alternative, the risk is that if the fight goes on long enough, this couple could end up being a part of the problem that they are now merely discussing.

A better alternative is for them to recognize as soon as it becomes evident that they are diametrically opposed on this issue. More important, since their opposition on the issue is based on diametrically opposed values, there is little or no chance that anything that either one could say would change the other's mind. As a matter of fact, the longer the discussion continues, the greater the chances that they will each become more firmly entrenched in their positions.

The tactic at this point is simply to agree to disagree and then to drop it! If you agree that it is really okay for you to see things differently, that is, that neither party will attempt to "convert" the other, the subject will be much safer to discuss in the future, should it arise again. In the meantime, both of you can get on with living (or working) together productively, since this point of difference can now be conveniently sidestepped.

It is highly unlikely that any two people involved in a long-term work or marital relationship will share all core values. Not to recognize this invites much needless hassling and arguing. Although there seems to be constant pressure on people in interdependent relationships to locate the common ground, there needs to be just as much effort devoted to isolating and honoring areas of irreconcilable differences. After all, these are just as natural and human as are the common-ground areas.

In these rare relationships that are extremely interdependent and long term, both parties could hold views and values that are so polarized that if either pursues his or her value, it will automatically create pain or severe problems for the other. Some examples of this are the need for autonomy versus the need for participation, the need for privacy versus the need for community, concern with production versus concern for people, and the need for isolation versus the need for intimacy.

When the situation is a blocking one with no common ground available and your respective positions are so far apart that any concession on your part will cause you to lose self-respect or self-esteem, consider the following procedure:

1. *Agree to disagree.* Establish the norm clearly that you both have a right to see it your individual way and that it is okay for the other person not to like it.

2. *Establish the importance of the relationship.* Alone or, if possible, together surface all the positive, productive aspects of the relationship. Get in touch with your commonly held core values and past successes. Resurface the happy times and the times when you gave each other solid support. Honor your potential for good work and support in the future if you can get through this issue. Find and fully acknowledge the real interdependent nature of your relationship; this will provide you with the support and incentive you need to get completion on the current problem. (Note that this step might also surface the possibility that you and the other person do not have enough going for you, and permanent disengagement may be the solution that would most benefit both of you.)

3. *Stick it out!* If you have determined that the relationship is important and well worth saving or working on, *stick it out!* Do not back away from your position if it is only to please the other person or reduce his or her pain. Be appreciative, but do not accept concessions that have been made to you for the same reasons. If your evaluation of the relationship has been correct, you will start to find ways to continue to work together productively, even though you are both experiencing some pain. Remember, just because you are in violent disagreement on this issue does not mean you disagree violently on all the other issues.

Working or living with someone under conditions of extreme disagreement is an incredibly heavy burden for both parties. Sooner or later, even if it is because of exhaustion, you are likely to mutually agree to "let go." More to the point, as the exhaustion increases, the importance of other issues and viewpoints changes as well. This will frequently bring you to a place of resolution. Remember, a roller coaster ride can be a lot of fun, or it can be absolutely terrifying. Either way, you don't get off until the ride is over!

Deal with What, Not Why

Almost all fights, creative or otherwise, arise from the fact that each party wants something different. In addition, compliance from the other person is usually necessary for the attainment of the objective. You need to get clear on *what* the other party wants, particularly in terms of how it differs from what you want. However, it is at best a total waste of time and at worst an invitation to a psychological slugfest to spend time and energy exploring *why* the other person wants what he wants.

As stated earlier, people have a right to want what they want and to want all of it. This point is tremendously relevant to creative fighting. When you respond to your opponent's question "Why do you want that?" you subtly place yourself in the role of defendant and your opponent in the role of judge, that is, your opponent is now in a position to decide how worthy your reason is. Although you may be strongly tempted to explain your motivation, since this is a golden opportunity to convince your opponent, and to do it at your opponent's invitation, your opponent will usually find your response anything but convincing.

Consider the following interchange between Carmen and Pat:

C: Pat, I'd like you to change your position on the report.
P: Why do you want that?
C: Because a change will allow me a more active role in the project.
P: Why do you want a more active role?
C: Well, I feel underutilized as things stand right now.
P: Why do you feel that way?
C: I don't know. It's just like when I was a kid. I'd get most of the good ideas and my older brother would end up getting all the credit. Are you going to change it?
P: No.
C: Why not?
P: We've always used this approach.
C: Why's that?
P: The boss's son instituted it.
C: Why is that so important?
P: The kid has done a lot of good work here and really has the old man's ear. Now do you understand why I can't help you?
C: No.

Several things are apparent in this hypothetical dialogue. First, in both cases the individual who was explaining her position was one down. With each "Why?" she had to reach farther and farther down to come up with an explanation or a justification. Second, with each transaction the conversation got further away from the salient issue, that is, the report. With each "Why?" and "Because," the thrust became more focused on defending the original position, rather than on dealing with the problem. Third, both parties are in a stance of defensiveness, each being frustrated by the other. If this particular issue does not result in a fight, at the least the potential for one later on has been increased.

The strategy in all cases is to stay away from other people's motivations wherever possible. Very few people know why they want what they want all the time anyway. It is enough that they want it. The primary tactic coming out of this strategy is to keep all your energy focused on what is available and how to get it. For example:

C: Pat, I'd like you to change your position on the report.
P: Why do you want that?
C: Because I want a more active role on the project and a change will give me that.
P: Why do you want a more active role?
C: What's your objection to helping me?
P: I'm vulnerable. The boss's kid instituted the current approach.
C: I want to get together with you to see if we can figure out a way for me to get more involved in the project without putting you on the line at the same time.

In this example, Carmen stopped the why–because cycle by asking Pat what the *current* objections to granting her request were. By focusing on what was happening rather than on why it was happening, the *real* issues surfaced and could be responded to—that is, not the report but involvement in the project for Carmen and vulnerability for Pat.

Laugh If It's Funny

Fighting, creative or otherwise, is most often viewed as a grim and serious business. In many cases, of course, it really is and certainly deserves to be respected. In many other cases, however, even when the subject of the fight is important and tempers are aroused, other things are occurring in the arena at the same time. Too frequently people lock themselves into the *form* of the fight rather than into the *substance*, and in so doing, they lose perspective. The longer the fight goes on, the more "serious" it becomes. The approach in creative fighting is to retain your perspective as much as possible, and humor is one of the best ways to do this.

Not too long ago, my wife and I got into a heated discussion over a relatively minor issue. It must have been one of those days when we both just felt like a good fight, because it wasn't long before the discussion had degenerated into a major confrontation. Brows were furrowed, shouts were heard, and tempers and nostrils flared! At the height of the battle my wife leveled a particularly devastating blow, turned away, hesitated, turned back to me and shouted, "Not only *that*, but you never really liked my mother!"

This stopped me cold, as my wife's reference to her mother had absolutely nothing to do with the argument. I looked at her, and her puzzled expression clearly said, "I can't believe I just said that." After another two or three seconds of stunned silence, the fight disintegrated into uncontrolled laughter.

The phenomenon here is that as the arguing time increases, so does the nobility of the cause and the righteousness of the arguers. You have to remember that along with the fight, there are a lot of other things occurring at the same time, and some of them are funny. Most people don't realize that along with being scary, fighting also has a potential for being amusing. As a matter of fact, slapstick humor is based on this premise. The trick, I have found, is to take the fight seriously but to avoid doing the same with myself.

CHAPTER 10

The Adversary Relationship Defined

Italians hate Yugoslavs;
South Africans hate the Dutch;
And I don't like anybody very much.
                                    —*Kingston Trio*

Much of the unnecessary stress and mess that arise from organizational conflict, whether in the industrial or the home setting, are centered in the concept of the natural adversary. Although conflict is positive when managed effectively, the concept of the natural adversary is destructive. It sets the stage for engaging in combat for the sake of combat, instead of engaging in it in order to obtain personal or organizational objectives.

Is the "Natural" Adversary Relationship Really Natural?

The natural adversary concept, which many people accept automatically, presupposes that simply because you are who you are and I am who I am, we will tend to be in perpetual conflict. When people believe this, one very costly result is that much energy is spent in constantly avoiding conflict rather than in finding ways to work and live together productively. Also, regardless of the cause, belief in the natural adversary condition becomes a self-fulfilling prophecy. That is, if you and I *expect* to conflict with each other simply because we belong to different groups, we will tend to behave toward each other in ways that make conflict unavoidable. When conflict eventually does occur, we have "proven" our theory, and it now becomes the norm. Each subsequent encounter more firmly establishes the appearance of the reality that we are, in fact, natural enemies.

It is my contention that there is nothing natural in this type of relationship. Furthermore, I think that it is a learned response and that it can be avoided by having a little awareness and by using conscious choice.

In its most basic form, the concept of the natural adversary seems well founded. There are many historical and literary references that point to the existence of the natural adversary relationship. The Montagues and the Capulets, and the Hatfields and the McCoys are examples of families who were eager to kill each other for no other reason than that the tradition for feuding called for it. We talk about fighting like cats and dogs and playing cat and mouse, and we refer politically to the hawks and the doves. The reality is, as anyone who owns both a dog and a cat will tell you, that these animals find a way to coexist in a supportive environment. In fact, we once had an old laboratory white rat and a kitten as pets. Although not the best of friends, they managed to survive and prosper in the same environment. The point is that even though many animals are instinctively predatory, they do not always attack other animals, and under the right conditions they will coexist peacefully with animals presumed to be their natural enemies.

As for humans as a species, I certainly concur with those who hold that humans have a propensity for violence and possess a predatory side. In primitive times there were no Burger Kings, and we had to hunt and avoid being hunted in order to survive. However, it is important that we keep in mind that those traits that characterize us as hunters are just several of the aspects that make up our individual personalities. Although each person has the *capacity for* violence, combat, and hostility, each person also has the capacity for their polar opposites: compassion, harmony, and supportiveness. What separates us from all other creatures is our ability to be consciously aware of each situation that we encounter and to allow that awareness to guide us toward consciously choosing the appropriate response each time. Although we may perceive of some adversary relationships as being natural, they are not! Thus neither I nor you are the *natural* adversary of any other human being. If two people are adversaries, it is strictly by *choice*. In many instances we find ourselves in adversary positions with other people both at work and at home. This is fine in that we all have different needs and wants at different times. The potential for damage begins when an adversary position begins to turn into an adversary relationship.

The Adversary Relationship in American Culture

Acceptance of the concept of the adversary relationship is fairly common in most Western cultures, but nowhere is it more ingrained than on the American scene. The stage for this was set at our birth as a nation and is an identifying characteristic of our Constitution. For example, the checks and balances system that was incorporated in the Constitution was intentionally designed to ensure that the separate parts of the federal government—the executive, the judicial, and the legislative branches—each had a means of blocking the others in order to avoid a concentration of power in one part.

Our brand of democracy supports and perpetuates the adversary relationship. When 51 percent of the population are getting what they want, the other 49 percent frequently are not. Party lines are always drawn between Democrats and Republicans, and even the party in power must constantly maintain its adversary stance, because there is always another election just around the corner.

With the adversary condition so ingrained in our national heritage, it is small wonder that the concept filters down into our daily existence. One has only to look around to see the hundreds of examples that point to the pride we take in incorporating the adversary relationship into our national identity.

Our heroes are lean, steely-eyed individualists who adhered religiously to the "code of the West." They shot first and asked questions later. What little boy didn't grow up playing cowboys and Indians or cops and robbers? We have an enormous love for competitive sports. Where most countries have one national sport, we have three. It is rare that the heavyweight champion of the world is not an American. I think we accord more honor to Super Bowl Sunday than we do to Christmas or Easter.

We acknowledge our poets but identify with our gunslingers! Although we authentically advocate peace, we have somehow managed to find ourselves at war approximately every 20 years since our birth some 200 hundred years ago. By way of contrast, Switzerland and Sweden haven't fired a shot at anybody in the same 200 years.

Make no mistake, I believe that no nation in the world has made more positive impact, been more effective, or displayed more genuine goodwill than we have, and this is due in part to our competitive approach to conflict. Rooting for the underdog is as much a part of being American as is any other of our identifying characteristics. The point is that whether we root for the underdog or for the topdog, we tend, almost reflexively, to see the other as an adversary and choose sides as a matter of course.

Although much that is positive emanates from this typically American orientation toward the adversary condition, there is certainly much that is negative as well. The biggest problem associated with this view is that whenever we adopt an adversary relationship between ourselves and others, we are responding to group similarities rather than individual differences and thereby risk a major loss of power. To be specific, if my first impression of you is that you are "one of them," there is a good chance that I won't get much past that point of view. I now deal with you as if this were the *only* identifying characteristic that you have as an individual, and we are back into the self-fulfilling prophecy that we are natural enemies. In effect, casting ourselves in an adversary relationship with others represents a loss of awareness, which, as mentioned earlier, is extremely destructive to contact and power.

To illustrate the point, suppose we were to randomly select five male master sergeants with 20 years' service and then choose five female first-grade teachers under the age of 30. I freely admit that there would be some startling differences between the two groups. However, I contend that there are many more differences among the sergeants and among the teachers than there are between them. By developing a stereotype of what sergeants are like and then assuming that all sergeants match this model, you are still responding to stereotypes of a group rather than individual differences. Once you lose awareness of any person's individuality you lose contact with that person. Once loss of contact occurs loss of power follows.

Distinguishing Characteristics of the Adversary Relationship

To understand the adversary relationship, there are several things that you need to consider that give this condition its unique identity. Also, adversary relationships must be distinguished from other types of negative relationships so that the options and conditions may be seen more clearly.

The primary objective in eliminating an adversary relationship is *not* to have the respective parties suddenly want to get along well. The primary objective is to restructure and normalize the relationship so that the conflict can be productive and fighting can be engaged in fully, openly, and creatively. If there is a potential for a more positive working relationship to develop among the adversaries, it can come about only if the process is addressed realistically and is then given all the time that it needs.

The adversary relationship is, after all, nothing more than a particularly nasty and toxic form of conflict. It does, however, differ greatly from the more common forms of conflict that are experienced in most family and work situations. There are at least six characteristics that differentiate adversary relationships from other varieties of nonproductive conflict.

First, other forms of nonproductive conflict are almost always based on misperceptions about issues. Adversary relationships are almost exclusively concerned with misperceptions about people.

Second, most nonproductive conflict is usually the result of poor contact. That is, things have been said badly, points have been made poorly, people have been unwilling to listen, or issues have not surfaced clearly. Adversary relationships are the product of no contact. Even when circumstances force the parties to engage, such as in arbitration, there is usually collusion between the parties to say as little as possible and to maintain as much distance from each other as the situation allows.

Third, other forms of nonproductive conflict are basically acute and are generally experienced as uncomfortable. A situation occurs, tempers flare, and the opponents are upset with the situation and with each other. Adversary relationships are chronic. There is a long-standing tradition for holding this view of the adversary and a desire to keep this view intact. Not only are the adversaries comfortable with the situation, in many cases it gives them a reason for being.

Fourth, the setting for other types of conflict is usually one of interdependence. That is, the conflict is occurring between individuals who have some need for each other and who may, at one time or another, have even shared a supportive relationship. In the adversary relationship, both parties tend to see each other as not now, and not ever, being of any use to each other or to the organization.

Fifth, it is possible to walk away from most nonproductive conflict with this acknowledgment: "This is the way it was, but now we have to find a new way to go because the situation has changed." That is, the conflict can be set aside by mutual agreement, and energy can be redirected toward more productive mutual outcomes. In adversary relationships the myths and negative stereotypes about the adversaries are usually so deeply rooted that they must be addressed and worked with before any permanent progress can be made.

Sixth, and the most destructive characteristic, in other forms of nonproductive conflict the desired outcome is still cast in terms of getting something that is wanted. Even though the conflict may not be progressing well, the worst that each opponent wishes is that he'll win and his opponent will lose. In the adversary relationship the desired outcome is to injure or destroy the adversary if at all possible.

The most obvious manifestations of the concept of adversary relationships are seen in religious, racial, and sexual prejudice. These varieties of prejudice carry the additional characteristic of extreme ill intent with them. In some ways, the gross stereotyping involved here, although the most vicious and destructive, is also the easiest to combat. Most people will not admit to this type of prejudice unless they are certain that they are with others who share the same view. Also, there is much legislation that counteracts the discrimination that would otherwise come from the natural adversary stance of these forms of prejudice—civil rights, equal employment opportunity and fair-housing laws, busing legislation, and so on.

In today's organizations there are many examples of the adversary relationship that, although not as vicious as racial prejudice, still hold a high potential for productivity loss and destructive conflict. One of the more obvious examples is the old-versus-young conflict. On the one hand, we have the veteran worker or supervisor whose basic view is, "Hell, it's not like when I was a boy. These kids just don't value work today!" This is counterbalanced by the younger worker or supervisor whose initial reaction is, "These old geezers are doing it the same way they did it 30 years ago. You can't teach them anything!" Although both perceptions may be accurate to some degree, the problem is that each group sees the other's identifying characteristic (age) as blocking what is wanted, rather than as a potential unknown resource. This problem is just as common in the home setting when communication problems between parents and teenage children set in.

Another arena for battle among natural adversaries is the organizational chart. Here the battle lines are drawn in the form of little boxes and little dotted lines. Manufacturing doesn't trust sales and marketing, finance and R&D are in perpetual conflict, and *nobody* can even talk to the people in data processing because they're a different breed of cat altogether!

Probably the most traditional adversary relationship in the organizational setting is between labor and management. The whole field of industrial relations sprang up in order to find ways to bring these two groups together. Nowhere is there a greater expectation for mistrust, hostility, and stereotypical behavior than at the bargaining table.

Whether the contact is between Turkey and Greece, the United Auto Workers and General Motors, the administration and the faculty, or parent and child, as long as the adversary relationship is cast in terms of *group* identity, rather than *individual* identities, the problem will be perpetuated.

Structure and Control of Interpersonal Relationships

Adversary relationships come in an infinite variety. Very few of these actually involve ill will in the beginning of the relationship. The ill will generally results from one or both parties' inability to deal effectively with real differences. Examples of these adversary relationships are: parent and child, supervisor and worker, even male and female.

I have said something about the American culture and the nature of Americans that predispose us toward developing adversary relationships. However, most adversary relationships among people in organizations and families and among other people who are interdependent develop because of a misalignment among the factors that formulate the interpersonal working relationships of the organizations and the control mechanisms that govern them.

The factors that formulate the structure of interpersonal relationships are principles, rules, and discipline. The control mechanisms that govern these relationships are power and authority. Before we look at the issues that contribute to causing adversary relationships, brief explanations of these five elements may be helpful.

1. *Principles* are statements of ideal values or conditions—for example, Honesty is the best policy; and The span of control should not exceed six, that is, there should be no more than six people reporting to a single supervisor. The function of a principle is to uniquely identify the individual or the organization and set boundaries that allow for deviation while pursuing the objectives. A principle sets a subboundary with clear polar opposites that encourages the individual to make free, conscious choices that will be effective without violating the spirit of the principle itself.

One of the most dangerous ways of applying a principle is to make it into an objective itself instead of using it as a guideline for appropriate behavior. When this occurs, the principle then demands rigid, inflexible behavior that will at best reduce effectiveness and at worst destroy effectiveness completely. If the principle in question states,

"The span of control should not exceed six," you can probably expand that number to eight or ten if conditions demand it. And although honesty is a good value under most circumstances, there are times when you might like to have an alternative available. A barracks mate of mine in the army was totally committed to the principle that honesty is the best policy. When a buddy showed him a picture of his new bride and proudly asked, "What do you think?" old Mr. Honesty got the opportunity to spend a couple of days in the infirmary to contemplate the wisdom of always being totally honest.

In sum, a principle serves the same function for people as a lighthouse serves for ships. The lighthouse marks the dangerous areas and acts as a navigational device so that ships can continue on their way safely and accurately. It does *not* say, "Come into the harbor, tie up, and never leave!"

2. *Rules* are statements that prohibit behaviors that will directly violate a principle. In effect, a rule translates principles into actions by setting the outer limit on what is or is not acceptable. For a rule to be effective, it must be *observably* in service to a clearly stated principle. Second, it must be flexible and responsive to the constantly changing conditions in which the principle operates. Third, both those obligated to conform to it and those obligated to enforce it must see it as reasonable and functional.

To illustrate, if the principle is that people must be able to travel safely, speed limits that are posted become one of the rules to carry out this principle. Note that the speed limits will change to reflect weather and road conditions or population densities and that under extreme circumstances they can even be situationally violated without penalty—for example, rushing an injured child to the emergency room.

3. *Discipline* is the legitimate sanctions that individuals are subject to for violating the rules. Discipline safeguards the existence of the principle by providing a *known* cost factor for breaking the rule. Discipline also provides an equitable and just means for dealing with a person who has broken a rule, without causing undue or unintentional damage to the individual or the organization.

For discipline to be effective and functional, it too must conform to certain standards. First, it must be consistent with the organization's principles concerning discipline—for example, one extreme might be, "Discipline should always be constructive," and the other would be, "An eye for an eye and a tooth for a tooth." The clearer the principle underlying the discipline, the easier it is to express the discipline in ways that are effective and consistent with the organization's character—for example, "Second-offense speeders go to school" as opposed to "Second-offense speeders go to jail." Note that the discipline is in the controlling of the offender's behavior, i.e., having to spend so much of his own time at a designated place. The learning which—it is hoped—will occur at the school is a separate, unrelated event.

Second, discipline must be consistent with and matched to the rule that has been violated. A first offense in breaking a critical safety regulation, for example, would seem to warrant a somewhat harsher disciplinary response than would a first-time lateness violation. In line with this, discipline should be graded. That is, the second infraction brings a harsher response than the first, and the third infraction brings a harsher response than the second. When dealing with issues of discipline, it is vital to keep in mind that it is *not* the function of disciplinary action to teach. The sole function of disciplinary action is to suppress unwanted behaviors. The time for teaching is when the rules are presented and discussed.

Third, the offender must see and experience the discipline as being just. Not only must the punishment fit the crime in terms of being a reasonable response to the infraction, but the offender must have been aware of what the risk was for committing the infraction prior to committing it. Although most of us are aware that ignorance of the law is no excuse, I can think of nothing that will create resentment more quickly than punishing an individual for an act that he did not know was a violation of a rule.

Fourth and probably most important, discipline must be expressed humanely rather than judicially. Thus the final imposition of the discipline is best left to the offender's immediate superior. By allowing the immediate superior to deal with the offender with as much personal discretion as the situation permits, the relationship between the superior and the subordinate is strengthened. And the immediate superior, being closest to the point of the infraction, is in a better position than any other member of the organization to decide what would be a fair outcome and to dispense that fair outcome.

Suppose that a company policy dictates that a third-offense lateness calls for a two-day layoff without pay and that both Paul and Larry are late for the third time. If Paul was late because his child was sick and Larry was late because he had a hangover, there is a clear need for different applications of discipline.

By encouraging the individual superior to deal with rule infractions with the broadest reasonable amount of discretion, the organization is helping her to do what she is there to do—directly manage and develop her own people. It is necessary to point out that when a manager chooses to deal with the discipline in a way that is inconsistent with the standard organizational policy, she is every bit as personally accountable for that choice as she is for a choice that conforms with organizational policy.

4. *Authority* is the right to attempt to get what you want in terms of organizational norms or objectives. Although frequently confused with power, authority is quite different and has its own set of identifying characteristics. First, the function of authority is to protect the integrity of the organization. Authority establishes smooth channels for communications and decision making and makes clear the differentiated roles and positions that make up the organization. Second, authority has its origin in the charter of the organization. Each position of authority is defined by the organization, which designates who is or is not subject to the specific demands of others—for example, I can tell my secretary what to do, but I can't tell your secretary what to do. Third, authority describes a position within a system but makes no reference to the individual who holds that position; in other words, a platoon sergeant is a platoon sergeant regardless of who is holding the position. Fourth, authority can be extended or limited in some cases by anyone who has greater line authority, that is, a higher-ranking line officer is in a position to supersede or countermand the order of a lower-ranking officer. Fifth, authority can be delegated.

Note that although authority is usually thought of in terms that describe a superior/subordinate relationship, it is not limited to that. A purchasing agent who has just been told that her ceiling on discretionary purchases has been raised from $5,000 to $10,000 has experienced an increase in authority just as much as has a supervisor who has just been promoted to general foreman.

5. *Power,* as discussed earlier and in contrast to authority, is the ability to get what you want in terms of organizational norms and objectives. It differs from authority on all points. Whereas authority resides in the organization, power resides in the individual. Whereas authority characterizes a position, power characterizes an individual. Whereas authority can be modified by those higher up in the system, power is solely an intrapersonal phenomenon and is not subject to external modification or delegation. Finally, where the function of authority is to maintain the structural integrity of the organization, the function of power is to attain organizational objectives.

The best way to see the distinction between authority and power is through contrasting the formal organization with the informal organization. The formal organization is a function of authority and is literally described by the charter and organizational chart. The formal organization accomplishes things through its stated rules and regulations, formalized objectives, policy statements, and established procedures.

The informal organization, on the other hand, is an invisible, unwritten structure that is based on power. The informal organization is made up of personal alliances among people that are based on friendship and/or mutual commitment to getting the job done. As the formal organization becomes larger, more rigid, and less responsive to individual needs and short-range goals, the informal organization is more heavily relied on to get things done. Where the basis for influence in the formal organization is credentials, in the informal organization the basis for influence is competence. In the formal organization people get things done through authority and established procedures; in the informal organization people get things done through wheeling and dealing, personal favors, and information flowing outside the established communication channels. Most of the change that occurs in the formal organization originates at the top; most of the change that occurs in the informal organization originates at the bottom.

Both organizations, the formal and the informal, serve specific needs and in some ways can be compared to the topdog–underdog dimension that was discussed in Chapter 5. In too many cases the formal organization will try to rout out the informal one by creating rules and regulations, procedures, and paperwork that limit personal contact and individual creativity. Similarly, in many cases the informal organization will attempt to subvert the formal one by ignoring, discounting, or sabotaging established effective and necessary procedures. A more productive approach would be for each organization to recognize the existence and contribution of the other and, where possible, to begin to collaborate with each other.

Organizational Causes of Adversary Relationships

Take a second look at the expression "natural adversary relationships." I pointed out that the word *natural* really isn't valid, since people have learned and adopted their adversary roles. The word *adversary* is appropriate, in that whenever we find ourselves in disagreement with others, we are truly in a situational adversary position with them. It is thus the word *relationship* that demands our attention so that we can be adversaries in this unique situation and not allow the situation to negatively influence the nature of the ongoing relationship.

Although an adversary relationship is chosen by the adversaries, it doesn't occur in a vacuum. There are several organizational variables that can contribute to the formation of these dysfunctional relationships. They usually have to do with the interplay of principles, rules, and discipline within the system, and reflect the roles of authority and power.

Disparity Between Principles

To begin to see more clearly how these negative relationships form, assume that an individual is joining an organization. This person has no prior relationship with anyone in the organization, and there is no cause for ill will on the part of the members toward the new person.

If the principles that define the organization are compatible with the new member's personal values, the first major source of problems is avoided. If, on the other hand, the organization and the individual have opposing principles and values, there is a reasonable probability that stress will begin to show in a relatively short period of time. Suppose that the organization is characterized by a high degree of openness among members and the new member places much value on keeping things to himself. There is a good chance that before long the new member will be seen by others as being sneaky, secretive, and uppity.

The adversary relationship forming in this case has its origins in the individual's and organization's holding mutually exclusive principles and values. This problem can be lessened or avoided by the organization's making its principles and values very clear during its recruiting and selection procedures and by its being equally clear about how much deviation it accepts and encourages. This will allow the individual and the organization to test and negotiate for compatibility before any commitments are made.

Principles, like values, can be categorized into four groups: (1) consonant—both parties hold values that are similar or compatible, (2) irrelevant—both parties hold values that are different, but this does not affect the living or working relationship, (3) disparate—the views are opposing, but they can be used as a basis for working out differences creatively, and (4) antagonistic—both parties hold mutually exclusive principles. It is only the last category that is a potential source of serious problems. Where possible, creation of such situations should be avoided.

Disparity Between Principle and Rule

Adversary relationships occur when the rules supporting a principle either no longer reflect the spirit of the principle or have themselves become totally self-serving. The function of rules is to support the principle in light of constantly changing conditions. If the conditions change and the rule does not, the result will be increasing resentment on the part of the individuals who must follow it and a deterioration in the relationship between those who are required to observe the rule and those who are required to enforce it.

Suppose there is a safety regulation that requires that a respirator be worn in a paint department because of the highly toxic nature of the paint solvents. There is no apparent problem in enforcing rigid adherence to the rule, since all parties can see the need for it. If, however, the paint department switches to a new line of water-based products and the rule does not change, each attempt to enforce the rule requiring respirators or to discipline someone for breaking it will be a step toward creating an adversary relationship.

Frequently, within families and organizations certain rules will be enforced to such an extent that a particular rule becomes an unquestioned law or tradition, such as attending religious services as a family each week. When this occurs, there is a potential for the development of adversary relationships. Rules that become traditions but that are not followed willingly or are simply not followed by all group members set the stage for adversary relationships developing between those who honor and enforce the tradition and those who do not but who have the rule imposed on them.

In one organization that I consulted with, a guiding principle was that people who work together should play together. There were many social events for the organization members and their families, and after a while an unwritten rule emerged that made attendance at these functions mandatory. Failure to attend a social event, without an excellent excuse, was considered an act of disloyalty and was arbitrarily interpreted as meaning that you really didn't care much about the company or your fellow workers. Although most employees followed the rule, some did so with a great deal of resentment, which clearly defeated the underlying intent of the principle.

Disparity Between Rule and Discipline

Attempting to enforce rules that countermand each other is, obviously, the first step toward organizational chaos. When discipline does not serve specific rules, it can become self-serving. At one extreme, institutions such as military academies are portrayed as environments whose sole purpose is to dispense discipline, regardless of need or cause. In Pat Conroy's classic novel *The Lords of Discipline*, life in a fictitious military college revolves around the central concept of discipline for its own sake. Not only are rules petty and unresponsive to principles, but a higher-status individual could impose discipline on a lower-status one simply as a whim. Other examples of this extreme position can be seen in hazing rituals in schools and social organizations, in codes of conduct in religious orders, and in such time-honored precepts as Spare the rod and spoil the child. At the other extreme are the individuals and groups who see any form of discipline as dehumanizing and as stifling the creative potential of the child or subordinate and therefore will not discipline under any circumstances.

It is certainly each individual's right to maintain a personal position on the value of discipline for its own sake. Regardless of what the value is, it is critical to keep in mind that unless the individual who is subject to the discipline is a solid supporter of the discipliner's values or principles, there is going to be trouble. In my experience, nothing will trigger the adversary relationship between two people more quickly than the administration of discipline without a clear, mutually seen cause and without just procedures. And if you want to turn a bad situation into an outright disaster, just accompany any form of discipline with a sanctimonious statement such as "I'm only doing this to you for your own good" or "You'll thank me for this later."

The Control Factors—Authority versus Power

Even when there is alignment among principles, rules, and discipline, problems can still occur, depending on which control factor, authority or power, is most influential. As I have mentioned earlier, both authority and power are essential to the survival and effectiveness of any organization. Authority maintains the structural integrity of the organization, and power gets things done. A good rule of thumb is that the more power and the less authority that are invoked, the lower the probability that there will be adversary relationships. That is, there is a direct cause-and-effect relationship between the reliance on authority to get things done and the occurrence of adversary relationships.

Holding the view that submission to authority is a virtue is very likely to contribute to the creation of the adversary relationship. The consistent and overriding contention in this book is that power—the ability to make conscious choices for yourself—is the *natural* state. When a ranking individual or an organization attempts to impose a value on people that ignores their growth needs and natural tendencies, there will be problems within the organization at some level, and adversary relationships will begin to form.

Many people make the mistake of conceptualizing virtues as *universally* held values. In fact, what is a virtue for one specific person or group may not be a virtue for another. For example, creativity is highly desirable in designers but not necessarily in bookkeepers. For a virtue to be valid as a goal or a standard of judgment, it must be consistent with the basic nature of the members of the organization or group, and it must also be *perceived* as a virtue by them—for example, the compassion of the clergy, the ferocity of prizefighters, and the attention to detail of brain surgeons. When a virtue is cast as appropriate for *all* individuals, regardless of their cultural or organizational identity, the virtue becomes a "should." When this occurs, people begin to try to conform to the virtue whether it is appropriate for them or not, with the inevitable result that they begin to become less powerful.

Submission to authority, as with any human value, can be very appropriate situationally, such as in combat conditions, crises, or where that particular value characterizes the organization *and* its voluntary membership. On the other hand, when submission to authority is enforced as a "must" for membership in an organization when it does not characterize the organization itself, the so-called virtue produces several highly negative conditions. First, it discounts its members' natural tendency toward freedom and independent action. Second, it demands that the leaders, or those in authority, *always* be right. Third, it sets the stage for low creativity, apathy, and potential rebellion. Fourth, and most important, it determines how conflict and rule violations will be dealt with. It is out of the fourth aspect that adversary relationships are born. That is, when submission to authority is held as an organizational virtue, any infraction of a rule is usually seen as a sin against the system, and the tendency then is to deal with the infraction as if it were a crime. This in turn sets up a much stronger tendency to use a judicial approach to dealing with infractions, that is, a prescribed punishment for a specific act, instead of a human approach, which encourages the immediate supervisor to weigh all relevant factors and then discipline as is appropriate to the unique situation.

Those who value authority for its own sake frequently use the statement "Do it because I say so," not "Do it because it needs to be done." Whenever a superior uses the first statement instead of the second, he has lost on two counts. First, the best that the superior (boss, supervisor, parent) can hope for is absolute *minimum* compliance with the demand. Second, the superior has chosen to rely on authority, rather than power, to get compliance, and in so doing, he has disempowered himself. That is, the next time the superior wants compliance from the same individual, he will probably not be able to get it without making an authoritarian demand.

In summary, there certainly are situations that call for authoritarian control either because of the extreme nature of the situation or because of the extreme resistance of the individual. Unfortunately, these conditions do not lessen the costs for using authority instead of power. However, when authority is inappropriately used to get things accomplished, the ultimate result is a slow but steady constriction of the family or the organization.

As a closing note on adversary relationships, I'd like to point out that some adversary relationships are unavoidable, despite the ideal that says there shouldn't be any. Suppose that as a result of current legislation prohibiting questions concerning race, religion, and political affiliation, three Ku Klux Klan members are hired in a department that is currently made up of 20 percent ethnic minority members. The potential is there for some very real conflict because the two subgroups will almost inevitably view each other as natural adversaries and have a strong emotional commitment to remaining adversaries. Fortunately, most of the adversary relationships that do exist, or that have a potential for existing, in the work or family setting are not this rigidly defined, predictable, or potentially volatile. For example, stepchildren can develop relationships that run the gamut from Cinderella to the Brady Bunch. The next chapter will discuss ways to deal with the adversary relationship.

CHAPTER 11

Contending with the Adversary Relationship

Over the years, I have noticed that the larger or more complex the organization, the more specialized the subdivisions—and the expertise of the individuals who make up the subdivisions. This technical specialization tends to produce strong subgroup identification, with the result that individuals often attach a high value to their own contributions, at the expense of the contributions of others. This leads to less contact among the various subgroups, particularly if they are competing for scarce resources.

Along with the distancing that occurs through technical specialization, there is also often conflict between people who handle line and staff functions. The primary function of staff managers is to support the line managers in allied areas such as personnel, payroll, and so on. Unfortunately, many times managers of line functions perceive that staff managers butt into areas that don't concern them, and staff personnel feel that line managers reject needed assistance and frustrate their efforts to do their job effectively.

It is important to be aware that even under generally good conditions adversary relationships can slowly develop between subgroups simply because of the size and structure of the organization. These adversary relationships will erode the power of the organization as people and subgroups become increasingly less willing to engage each other fully and deal with issues that affect the system's survival and growth.

In handling the adversary relationship, there are two strategies: avoiding it and dealing with it.

Avoiding the Adversary Relationship

The old bromide about an ounce of prevention being worth a pound of cure is never truer than in the case of adversary relationships. It is infinitely easier to avoid an adversary relationship than it is to deal with one already in progress. On a day-to-day basis the organizational causes discussed in Chapter 10 are probably the biggest contributing factors to the development of adversary relationships. And these causes are controllable if you maintain your awareness of what they are and how they work. There are several other pitfalls that you can avoid just by being aware of them.

Don't Breed Competition Within the Organization

Of all the managerial strategies and family philosophies that have produced internal horror, breeding competition among members is probably the most destructive. As mentioned, Americans are lovers of competition, and setting conditions in which internal units have to compete for scarce resources, prizes, or approval has been very popular. The thinking is that if we can get the salespeople or production units or academic departments or kids "jumping for the jelly beans," they will enjoy the work more, they will work harder and more efficiently, and the whole organization will become more involved and effective as a result. This approach heads my personal list of "Things That Seemed Like a Good Idea at the Time." In my experience, this strategy almost always has the opposite effects. Although I could cite endless examples, I'll share just two.

For my doctoral dissertation, I chose to study the motivational needs of industrial salesmen and was fortunate to have a large corporation invite me in to study 11 of their 43 national retail outlets. This gave me a sample of 175 salesmen from across the 11 companies. As I was putting the finishing touches on my plan for collecting the data I needed, I asked the president of the retail chain if I could get some information for him, over and above my data, since I had direct access to the sample. He was pleased with the offer and asked if I would find out how the national sales contest was being received by the salesmen. To avoid influencing the responses, I simply included the open-ended question "How do you see the company recognizing your efforts?" The idea was to see how many of the 175 participants would mention the program by name and then see what they had to say about it.

The results were mind-boggling! First, only 3 of the 175 people in the sample mentioned the contest. Second, one person mentioned it positively and two mentioned it negatively. And third, of the two who mentioned it negatively, one was last year's winner! What had made it a negative experience for him was that after he had been honored at the awards dinner and had been given the plaque and the prize, his sales manager did not come over to congratulate him.

Another example occurred during my early years of teaching in the department of management of a prominent southeastern university. A new incoming president of the university decided that it would be a good thing to set up competition among the schools and departments and announced his strategy to the faculty, using the euphemism of "providing creative tension." What his creative tension produced was divisiveness among the departments that had to work together, feelings of alienation among individuals, and a growing resentment toward him and his administration. The last I heard, he had been asked to resign.

Competition is neither good nor bad in and of itself. Competition is productive when its aim is proper, that is, at the organization or the individual that you are attempting to beat. The object of competition is to beat the other person. It is a destructive force that is appropriate under the right circumstances. It seems to me that it is never appropriate to turn a destructive force loose within one's own department.

Know What Behavior You Are Rewarding

Humans as a species learn faster and better than any other species. Learning starts at birth and ends at death and is most influenced by what is being used for rewards and punishments along the way.

In the work setting many institutional rewards and punishments are offered and used with the hope of controlling behavior. Some of the more obvious of these are pay, promotions, and bonuses on the reward side, and reprimands, written warnings, and suspension on the punishment side. I suppose that these complex and highly visible organizational rewards and punishments have some effect in the long run. However, they are by no means the most important or effective ones that can be used.

Much more potent in shaping behavior on the job and in the home are the scores of small rewards and punishments that are doled out in the normal course of working or living together. Remember the salesman who cared more about the sales manager's congratulations than he did about winning the national sales contest. Or take the youngster who has just done something to annoy his parent. Instead of pointing out why the behavior is inappropriate, the exasperated parent turns to the kid and says, "Why can't you be more like your brother?" Has a punishment been given? Oh, yes! Is this the very first seed of an adversary relationship? You bet! By the third time the comparison is made, it's a pretty safe bet that instead of trying to be more like his brother, the youngster is going to be developing some pretty deep-seated resentments toward him, and the adversary relationship is born. In this case, the brother hasn't even done anything to provoke an adversary relationship other than be himself. The parent (that is, the authority figure) has set the stage and the conditions for the adversary relationship to develop.

In the work setting the same type of unaware handling of reward and punishment goes on constantly. Who gets the first offer of over-time? Who does the boss tend to avoid at coffee breaks? Who gets more of the boss's time? Who is not asked for advice? These are all very subtle but very effective shapers of behavior.

As behavior changes, a shift in attitude almost always goes along with it. For example, if I succeed (behavior), I am going to feel more confident (attitude), and if I am yelled at (behavior) I am going to feel defensive (attitude). What makes the small rewards and punishments such powerful shapers of behavior and attitudes is that, first, they are occurring all the time, second, they are exactly matched to the event, and third, they occur immediately, thereby instantly reinforcing the particular behavior and its following attitude.

I am not suggesting that you plan out everything that you are going to say or do ahead of time, with the hope of avoiding these problems. It would be an impossible task, and if you were successful, you would lose all your spontaneity and thereby lose all your effectiveness. What I am suggesting is a few guidelines that will help you get more and easier control over the process.

Take the time to get clear about what it is that you really want from the other person. For example, do you really want the boy to be more like his brother, or do you want him to be more like himself but a little more appropriate in the process? The clearer you are about what you want from the other person, the easier and the more natural it will be for you to get it.

Be aware of what you are using for rewards and punishments. Don't sell yourself and your personal impact short. Just as you would probably prefer being well thought of and having the respect of your boss and parents, so would your subordinates and children. Although my approval of me is more important to me than your approval of me, this does not mean that your approval of me is unimportant!

Focus on equity rather than on equality. It isn't possible to give everybody equal amounts of everything. In fact, very few people want equal amounts of everything. One person would like a closer personal relationship, and another would prefer more autonomy; one person feels the need for more direction, and another has a need for more independence. Take the time to find out what your people (including your kids) want and don't want, and start to use *these* as a basis for rewards. As long as a person is getting what she or he wants, it doesn't matter very much what someone else is getting.

Focus on rewards rather than on punishment. There are clearly times when punishment is appropriate, but these times are very few and far between. Remember that people do not learn positive behaviors through punishment! They do learn positive behaviors through rewards. The function of punishment is to stop an unwanted, known behavior. If you don't punish inappropriately, you won't risk resentment, which is the basis of the adversary relationship.

Finally, do not compare your subordinates or your children with each other. Wanting a youngster to be more like his brother creates animosity and resentment. If you are going to use comparison, compare the individual's former behavior with his current behavior in the light of clear external criteria or standards. In taking this approach, you heighten the other's awareness of the standard for preferred behavior, you facilitate his taking responsibility for his own behavior, and you get him to address the specific behavior without resentment. People resent other people, they never resent themselves.

Don't Dehumanize the Adversary

Dehumanization is the process of attempting to rob someone of her dignity and make her seem less than human in her own eyes. This is usually attempted through such things as sarcasm, physical beating, slurs and stereotypes, derision, disenfranchisement, nonresponse, and removing options. The function of dehumanization is to give the other person the message: "You do not exist." Nothing evokes more rage and permanent interpersonal hatred than this.

In looking at the world today, I am absolutely convinced that World War III is inevitable. But it won't be fought between the East and the West, as most political observers might anticipate. It will be waged between the smokers and the nonsmokers of this planet!

As a smoker who travels a lot, I realize that smoking does cause discomfort to some nonsmokers. I had no objections when the airlines split the cabins into smoking and nonsmoking sections. After all, I'm a reasonable guy and I realize that we do have to make some accommodations so that we can all live together. Last week, on a two-and-a-half-hour flight to Dallas, the steward announced that the flight was full and that since the Civil Aeronautics Board guarantees a no-smoking seat to all passengers, there would be no smoking for the duration of the flight. Goodbye, reasonable guy! Hello, natural adversary! A very pleasant elderly lady was sitting next to me (not smoking, of course), and I found myself wondering, very hostilely, "Was she the one?"

The issue here is really not one of smoking or not smoking. After all, when I go to a movie or to the theater, I can't smoke there either. What really made the difference in this incident was that I was clearly told by the CAB and by the airline that I did not exist. In a movie I can go to the lobby for a smoke if I choose to, and at the theater there are intermissions. In these cases, where no smoking is the rule, some provision is made so that I can take care of myself.

Policies and rules that are instituted for the betterment of the organization and its members will sometimes favor one group over another. Take the time to see whether this is the case, and if it is, make sure that the outgroups' needs are somehow acknowledged and at least minimally provided for.

Keep the Work Meaningful

One of the best ways to lessen the probability that adversary relationships will develop is to focus on the work, not on the relationships. There is a raft of literature that points to the inescapable conclusion that motivation is an internal process. People are motivated when they are doing something because they want to do it. Pay, fringe benefits, and the other material rewards used in the organization really have nothing to do with human motivation. The wise manager will keep a constant eye out for any opportunity to restructure a job or a task so that it will provide the employee with more challenge, more fun, greater responsibility, or an opportunity to learn something new.

Attending to the motivation needs of subordinate managers and workers naturally provides its own rewards, in terms of higher productivity, less waste, greater worker satisfaction, and so on. The absence of the motivating factors in jobs does not automatically result in adversary relationships. But what does result is the development of a breeding ground for adversary relationships. The less there is in a job to draw the interest and energy of the employee, the more time the employee has to reflect on insults, injuries, and past injustices. The duller the work, the more pain there is to be perceived, and the more leisure time there is in which to perceive it. Faced with boring, meaningless work for an indefinite period, you can always scare up plots, cabals, and "bad guys" for lack of anything better to do.

Dealing with the Adversary Relationship

There are no simple or easy steps to ensure a positive outcome to an adversary relationship. Each adversary relationship is unique and is usually grounded in its own particular tangle of historical events and misperceptions. Adversary relationships have different origins and vary in intensity. In milder cases, however, it is usually quite helpful to bring in a third party to facilitate and maintain control of the process.

In dealing with adversary relationships, it is possible to identify three different roles. First is the role of adversary, played by the people in conflict. Second is the role of peacemaker, that is, a person who is not an adversary but wants the relationship resolved, such as a boss or a parent. Third is the role of facilitator, the person who actively works with the adversaries in an attempt to help them to restructure their relationship along more positive lines. It is possible for an individual to occupy more than one of these roles. For example, a boss who wants two subordinates to better their relationship might also have the skills to facilitate the process and choose to do so. Or the adversaries themselves might choose to restructure their relationship and thus take on the peacemaker role and seek out a facilitator on their own.

For the purposes of clarity, this section is directed to the facilitator who wishes to help the parties in conflict resolve their adversary relationship. However, most of the ideas can also be used by the adversaries themselves if they elect to proceed without a facilitator.

If you are going to address the relationship, there are five steps in which control can be exerted in order to make the process more workable. The function of these five steps is to get the relationship in a position where the basic ground rules for constructive conflict and creative fighting will become operational.

Step 1. Both Parties Decide That They Want to Change the Relationship

Although many adversary relationships seem to be the result of organizational inconsistencies, the fact is that no matter what the cause or how objective the factors seem to be, the adversary relationship is always totally subjective. That is, the involved parties are deeply, emotionally, and personally committed to maintaining it. I would even say that in many, if not most, cases the event that originally precipitated the relationship was some form of insult or personal slight.

What makes the adversary relationship so difficult to work with is that, along with being steeped in tradition and personal identification, the relationship is almost impervious to contact. Before there can be any actual engagement between the adversaries, both parties must see an advantage to changing the situation.

Step 2.   *Consider a Facilitator*

It is sometimes a good move to consider using a third party or a facilitator to work with the adversaries and the process. Since it's a fairly safe bet that at the outset neither party is particularly willing to listen to what the other has to say, having someone on the scene that both parties are willing to listen to can be a tremendous help. It is also unlikely that either party has the contact skills that are needed to work out the relationship productively. (If they had these skills, there probably wouldn't be an adversary relationship in the first place.)

A facilitator can be brought into the process either by the peacemaker, who wants the relationship resolved, or by the adversaries themselves. For example, suppose that a manager is experiencing problems arising from an adversary relationship between two of his subordinates. He can discuss the problem with a consultant first, and then suggest to the adversaries that some work on the relationship might be helpful. Or members of a family might find themselves taking extreme positions and choose to seek out some professional counseling to help them deal with each other more contactfully. There are myriad ways that a facilitator may be brought in. It is of critical importance that the final decision of whether to use a facilitator, and who that person should be, rests with the adversaries.

Someone acceptable to both adversaries may be a consultant, a member of the clergy, or an impartial friend. Even if the facilitator is not to be used initially, it's wise to have him or her in the wings in case there is a sudden need or deadlock.

The individual who is chosen as the facilitator should (1) be seen as a friend to both sides or be seen as neutral by both sides, (2) have no personal investment in the outcome, (3) have good contact skills, (4) have some experience, or at least no discomfort, working with conflict, (5) have some degree of commitment to a positive outcome regardless of what that outcome might be, and (6) be reasonably patient.

The second step is to fully inform the facilitator about the existing situation. At this point the focus of the work is to bring the facilitator in as part of the process. It is helpful for the facilitator to be aware of such things as the specific nature of the relationship, the duration of the relationship, what damage has been done and to whom, and who initiated the need to change the relationship (for example, was it one of the involved parties or a peacemaker, such as a boss or parent?).

The third step is usually to have the facilitator meet with both adversaries. Whether the facilitator meets separately with each adversary or with both together will be determined by how intense the adversary relationship is. It is my experience that in most work settings the meeting is generally with both adversaries together because that is the norm in most business environments, where at least the pretense of objectivity is sought. On the other hand, adversary relationships between teenage children and their parents are more often handled by the facilitator meeting separately with the teenager and the parents. The best and easiest way to go is to simply encourage the adversaries to meet together unless they prefer not to. Each situation must be judged independently. This is the most important step for the facilitator because it is here that the supportive relationships between the facilitator and the adversaries are established. During the initial meeting with adversaries, the first thing that the facilitator must do is to establish a contract for how he will work with them. If this was not done when the facilitator was brought into the process, it must be done at this time. If either or both adversaries begin to mistrust or to lose trust in the facilitator during the process, the whole project fails and this failure will leave the situation between the adversaries worse than it was before.

Some elements that it is important for the facilitator to get agreement upon from both parties are:

1. The facilitator will respect the confidentiality of anything that is said. This means that the facilitator will repeat nothing said to anyone in confidence without the explicit permission of the person who made the disclosure.

2. The facilitator has the right to refuse to act as a go-between. Although the situation may call for the facilitator to carry messages between the adversaries during the early stages, the facilitator's primary role is to facilitate direct contact between the parties involved. The facilitator cannot allow her role to turn into yet another buffer that encourages the parties to avoid dealing with each other face to face.

3. The facilitator will not take sides. The facilitator can state an understanding of a particular position or even acknowledge how that

position might be painful for the individual involved. The moment the facilitator agrees with or supports any position, the neutrality and power of the third-party position is destroyed and the game is lost.

4. The facilitator's personal opinion may be stated. There is no question that the facilitator will form opinions as things progress. If it is helpful for the facilitator to state an opinion, it has to be just that and not be interpreted as a judgment or an alliance. Suppose that during the process one party makes a statement that is patently absurd. By remaining silent, the facilitator colludes with the individual by appearing to believe that the absurd point is legitimate. One of the facilitator's contributions to the process is to act as a sounding board for the adversaries. Incidentally, an adversary is under no obligation to agree with any point made by the facilitator.

Once the contract has been established between the facilitator and each adversary, the facilitator begins to assist each adversary in getting clearer about his position. The clearer each party is, the greater the likelihood of an eventual positive outcome. Some of the areas of concern that the facilitator can assist the adversary in becoming clearer about are: (1) what the other party is like, (2) the advantages of keeping things the way they are, (3) the current conditions that might be improved if there were a change, (4) the things that the adversary fears might happen if the relationship were to take a more positive direction.

Step 3.   Clarify Positions

Although it is always wise to avoid issues of morality when engaging in any conflict, it is absolutely vital to avoid these issues when dealing with natural adversary relationships. The relationship may have its origins in a conflict over morals or values. But any move to address these issues will escalate, not diminish, the conflict.

In an attempt to break the adversary relationship, the initial emphasis is usually placed on getting both parties to see the error of their ways. Although this approach probably works in some instances, when you attempt to get the adversaries to each see that they have been wrong, they will be likely to defend their respective positions and to resist any attempt to modify them.

If both parties are willing to attempt to resolve the situation, there is an alternative approach. My view is that the adversary relationship is the dominant factor, but something has occurred in the environment that has made both parties feel that it would be appropriate for them to explore the possibility of working toward a resolution. Both these elements must be honored; that is, the relationship is what it is *and* something has changed. The first step in breaking the adversary relationship is to acknowledge the relationship and honor it *as it is*. That is, do not make any attempt to find a common ground or to change the perception of either party at first. Instead, legitimize each party's right to see things the way he sees them. (Remember that in the beginning both parties will see things in their own way anyway, regardless of who says they should or shouldn't.) By legitimizing both parties' right to see the situation the way that they see it, you ensure that neither party has to invest any energy in defending his known position.

Now that there is an established norm for both parties to have a right to different views, the second step is to have each party state his position as clearly as the situation will allow. Although usually the opponents' full disclosure of their respective views is desirable, some adversary relationships may be so volatile that an initial full disclosure would be counterproductive. Encourage the adversaries to disclose only as much as they feel safe disclosing, keeping in mind that anything they say is likely to be interpreted literally, with no leeway given for inaccuracy or overstatement. This situation can be very threatening, so you need to do all you can to make the environment as safe as possible. The point here is that the clearer each party is about how the adversary sees the relationship and its implications *before* the two of them attempt to reconcile their differences, the higher the probability that they will make progress once actual engagement occurs.

To illustrate, some years back I did a fair amount of work with groups on the issue of race relations inside organizations. Although the stated purpose of the work was to deal with discrimination, in several instances the groups chose to work on the gut issue of prejudice. The process that I used to work with these groups was as follows:

1. We established the norm that for the duration of the program it was okay to be prejudiced and to own up to it. We accomplished this by discussing the reality that if the issue was one of literally prejudging other people, we were probably all doing it to some extent. We simply needed to recognize and legitimize what was actually going on at the time.

2. I asked the group to split into two groups, one white and the other black, and to put as much physical distance between them as the room allowed. It was interesting to note that on several occasions some whites joined the black group out of a sense of identity with them.

3. Each group was asked to generate two lists of adjectives. The

first list was to be in response to the question "What are *they* like?" The second was to be in response to the question "What will *they* say that *we* are like?"

4. I asked both groups to make their lists public. If the white group asked to disclose their "What are *they* like?" list first, I then asked the black group to disclose their "What will *they* say that *we* are like?" list. The lists were compared and then the process was reversed.

Both groups' lists of "What are *they* like?" were more positive and better balanced than their lists of "What will *they* say that *we* are like?" That is, both groups had a more balanced and fairer view of the other group than the other group guessed that they would have.

This exercise taught me that whether the adversary relationship is between individuals or between groups, both sides are going to be very concerned about how they are seen by each other. The tendency in prolonged natural adversary relationships is to focus only on the negative aspects of the other group or person, and therefore to assume that the other is doing the same.

If there is value in starting from a *known* position rather than from a myth, this must include the positive as well as the negative perceptions. In the example just described, I had the groups use the specific technique of making "You are . . ." statements in a highly controlled exercise. Both groups agreed that it would be okay for them to do this. However, when adversaries actually engage each other, it is highly recommended, if not essential, that they cast all perceptions and positions about each other in "I think . . ." or "My view is . . ." form rather than in the form "You are. . . ." In addition, as much as possible they must back up their statements with specific examples. At this point any perceived invasion by one or both parties could destroy the entire process and create more hostility and distancing than existed before.

For example, compare the potential effect of each of these statements:

> "You people are uncooperative and unconcerned, and you couldn't care less about anybody's problems except your own!"

> "We have not gotten the support that we have needed from you in the past. Let me give you several examples: . . . ."

The rule of thumb to use when one adversary states his initial position to the other adversary, is that neither adversary can tell the other how the other one is or what the other one sees or how the other one feels. In other words, I can't tell you how you are and you can't tell me what I see or how I feel. It is helpful to establish this guideline clearly before any actual engagement occurs. It's also a good idea to keep it in effect throughout the entire process.

Step 4. *Redefine Roles in the Light of Current Conditions*

Once the adversaries have agreed that they may both benefit from reevaluating the relationship (Step 1), have decided whether to use a facilitator (Step 2), and once both are relatively comfortable with their own positions and tolerant of the other's (Step 3), the next step is to redefine the roles in terms of what is going on right now.

Occasionally, outside events will lead to a need for collaboration that is so compelling that it will be immediately apparent to both parties—for example, a sudden and unexpected attack from a third party (such as the collaboration that occurred among the various Yugoslav political partisans to fight the Nazi invasion) or the sudden opportunity for a mutual gain that would require immediate situational cooperation. In these unique situations, redefining the roles in light of the current circumstances may actually be the first step, not the fourth. That is, it may be possible for both parties to put past differences and perceptions on hold for the time being. This may be enough to get the adversaries working together quickly and effectively in response to the new condition.

After the crisis has been dealt with or the opportunity has been responded to successfully, the initial positions will still have to be addressed if any permanent progress is to occur. Although the immediate situation has been satisfactorily resolved, nothing has been done to deal with the initial misperceptions that each adversary holds about the other. You are back in the original position (Step 1) of checking to see whether both parties still want to change the nature of the adversary relationship. If they do want to, even though you have to start at the beginning, you are still to the good because there is now a successful collaborative experience that can be added to the history.

In most cases, the external condition that gets the adversaries to review their positions is not quite as dramatic as the ones just suggested. Usually, the situation is something that reflects a permanent or a long-range change in the environment, such as being bought out by a competitor, a change in command, your child's being bound and determined to marry that "loser," or suddenly finding out that your boss is going away for three weeks and leaving a disliked colleague in complete and total charge.

Redefining the roles according to the new prevailing conditions allows both parties to respond appropriately, without having to defend their former positions. As when you work with resistance, no progress is possible until each adversary is clear that his position (his resistance to contact) has been heard and acknowledged by the other. Once this has been established, your aim is to refocus the energy *away* from the initial positions that defined the adversary relationship and *toward* the new set of conditions that are drawing the adversaries to a more collaborative stance. This refocusing occurs in two areas: wants and concerns.

Wants. When you work with natural adversary relationships, there is little risk that confluence or compromise will emerge as the blocking factor to establishing a better-functioning relationship. The potential problem here is *invasion*. When the initial positions have been stated as clearly and as contactfully as possible, and there is mutual awareness that a less hostile stance might be to everyone's benefit, it is then appropriate for both adversaries to begin to look for a legitimate common ground. Often the best way to do this is by focusing on the adversaries' respective wants cast in terms of enlightened self-interest.

In the early stages of your work with an adversary relationship, an ongoing part of the process is the development of a minimal level of trust between the parties where none existed before. Both parties will always be doing some testing, but the testing is most critical at the start. The concept of *enlightened self-interest* dictates that the result of any collaborative effort can always be evaluated in terms of what each adversary is getting out of it personally, as well as in terms of what the benefits are to the family or the organization. In short, it is always legitimate for either party to say, "If I go along with this, what's in it for me?" Even more important, I must be able to see what's in it for you before I'll be willing to engage with you. If I can clearly see what you are going to get out of any collaborative effort with me, I can more readily trust both your suggestions and your objections. Altruism is nice, and wanting what is best for everybody is a noble philosophy and a lovely sentiment, but I suggest that you *never* use them as a basis for establishing a relationship between strangers or business contacts, let alone between adversaries.

Once each adversary is clear and not defensive about what he and his opponent want, it makes sense for them to come together in an attempt to develop mutual objectives and strategies that will achieve these ends.

Concerns. When you are redefining roles, it is also necessary to address what is *not* wanted by both parties if their attempt at collaboration is to be successful. Since each new situation holds equal potential for negative and positive outcomes, it is a good idea for the parties to be clear on what *new* concerns they have about what might occur as things progress.

There are certainly known risks when adversaries state their concerns to each other. The most obvious risk is that in doing this, one person is indicating where he is vulnerable, and the other person could take advantage of this information. On the other hand, if the person does not state a concern openly, he is back to keeping material bottled up and having it turn back into myth and negative stereotype, and he risks having his adversary inadvertently hurt him. After all, the adversary was unaware of this concern.

The most effective strategy is for the adversaries to state their concerns openly but cautiously. As with the open stating of wants, the open stating of concerns is a necessary part of establishing a minimal level of trust between the adversaries. This trust level is essential to restructuring the relationship in a more positive and permanent way. Note that the term *trust* translates into the statement "I will do nothing intentionally to harm you."

Step 5. *Develop a Contract*

Working on resolving a natural adversary relationship holds a great deal of potential risk, real or imagined, for both parties. The risk is even more pronounced because the engagement takes place in "uncharted waters," rather than in the old, familiar, and comfortable "combat zone." This new situation will heighten both parties' awareness of their own vulnerability.

One way to control the process and lessen the adversaries' sense of vulnerability is by using a contract. A *contract* is an informal agreement that is mutually negotiated *before* any actual work on the relationship is entered into by the adversaries. That is, developing the contract should be the *first* thing that they do together! (To avoid possible confusion, note that getting *clear* on positions and roles is done by both parties individually. This can be done by the facilitator working separately with each adversary at different times, or working with one adversary while the other observes. When possible, it always preferable to have the adversaries together).

If the adversary relationship is between two groups, one technique that works well in making positions known is called "The Fishbowl." In this technique, one group clusters in the center of the room, generally on the floor, and the other group sits on chairs encircling the first group. The group in the center is directed to talk among themselves about the way they see things, their wants, concerns, views of the other group, and so on. The witnessing group is required to remain silent and listen. Although provision can be made for the witnessing group to ask for clarification of a point if it is needed, they may not comment at all on anything that is said. When the first group is finished, the groups reverse roles and the process is repeated. When the parties actually meet with each other to work on these issues, it is done *after* a workable contract has been negotiated.

The purpose of the contract is to make clear the rules of the road that will guide the engagement throughout its course. The function of the contract is to get the process started and to allow it to proceed slowly. It does not lock the parties into a rigid set of behaviors; rather, it allows them to maintain control as things progress. The last element in any contract is a statement to the effect that the contract may be renegotiated at any time by mutual agreement.

Note that use of a contract is not restricted to engagements between adversaries. A contract is extremely helpful and appropriate in any situation in which people have to work together and have had little or no prior contact with each other. One of the very few inflexible rules of my professional life is to never conduct a training program or do a consulting job without first negotiating a contract with the individual or group. The contract fulfills several necessary functions. It provides the ground rules for the program so that both the participants and I have a good feel for what we can reasonably expect from each other. It also allows the participants to have a strong say and significant control over what will be happening, thereby avoiding unnecessary surprises. Most important, it allows the participants time and opportunity to experience me, as I am, before we engage in the work, as opposed to working with me from some preconceived notion of what I might be, or should be, like.

There are several advantages to taking the time to negotiate a contract when you are dealing with an adversary relationship. First, the contract clearly outlines what behaviors and actions will and will not be appropriate. This removes some points of vulnerability at the outset—for example, no name calling. Second, it provides the adversaries a clear, mutually agreed upon path for dealing with one another. Third, it provides a means for redress so that if a violation does occur, it can be dealt with specifically and the entire process won't be jeopardized. Fourth, the negotiation of the contract is a dry run for the entire engagement process. That is, the parties have to come together and state their wants and concerns openly in order to negotiate the contract.

Elements of the Contract. The contract needs to be flexible and responsive to the particular situation and the individuals involved. Most contracts should contain at least these five elements:

1. Purpose of the meeting or engagement.
2. Definition of areas of individual responsibility.
3. Agreed-upon guidelines for dealing with communications and conflict.
4. How demands will be made and answered.
5. Rules for disengagement.

Purpose of the meeting or engagement. It is practically impossible for any adversary relationship to be successfully resolved in a single meeting. More likely, in the first meeting neither party will be quite sure of what a successful outcome will look like when it is finally reached. The only thing that may be clear at the outset is that something needs to be done as soon as possible to change the existing relationship. Actually, as I mentioned before, this is a situation of exploring new territory rather than of getting from one known place to another.

Since this is the case, it is critical for the adversaries to address the *specific* objectives of *each* encounter at the beginning of each meeting and for these objectives to be agreed upon to everyone's mutual satisfaction. If the adversaries are going to make progress, they will have to make it in light of expectations that are reasonable in terms of both the time that is available and the degree to which they are willing to make commitments at this particular stage.

The statement of objectives can be quite formal, such as in a predistributed written agenda, or quite simple, such as the verbal statement "We're here to review past progress" or "To address the issue of bringing in an outside resource person to help us."

If the parties attempt to work from unreal or unclear expectations, the result will probably be more hostility and distancing than if the parties had not met in the first place. For example, "To put our differences aside and to work together for the betterment of all" is a nice long-term objective, but disaster is almost guaranteed if it is used as an objective of the first meeting.

Definition of individual areas of responsibility. It is the nature of adversary relationships for the opponents to blame each other for every screw-up that takes place. As soon as something goes haywire, either or both sides hurl cries of "Hell, you know how *he* is!" or "Isn't that just typical of *her*!" Clear definition of the areas of individual responsibility and agreement with them by the adversaries are essential before any work is undertaken. Each individual is totally responsible for getting or not getting what he wants. By making this point clear and having both parties see the value of it, you are making a big contribution to keeping the process running smoothly and avoiding "I told you so's" and blaming behaviors if and when something does go wrong.

Clear definition of the areas of individual responsibility heightens the opponents' awareness of boundary and demands of each participant that he take an active part in making sure that the meeting is moving along productively. Areas of responsibility involve issues such as boredom, annoyance, drifting off the subject, blithering, telling old war stories, and so forth. The agreement that you are seeking here is that anyone who becomes annoyed with what is going on accepts his obligation to indicate this as clearly and as contactfully as possible. Thus either or both parties can choose to stay bored or annoyed by what is happening at the moment, but if they do, it is their fault and not anyone else's. All parties to the meeting must take full responsibility for their own discomfort and for choosing or not choosing to live with it. Ideally, if someone is bored, he will say, "I am bored right now by what's going on, and I'm wondering if you are bored also."

Having each individual publicly agree to take care of himself during the meeting heightens each person's awareness that there is both an individual responsibility and a shared responsibility for the outcome of the engagement.

Agreed-upon guidelines for dealing with communications and conflict. As mentioned earlier, the natural adversary relationship is characterized by its absence of contact. In the early stages of engagement, it is sometimes best to formalize the rules of how the adversaries will communicate with each other. Obtaining agreement on such things as only speaking for oneself, addressing comments to a specific individual, speaking only in specifics, and not asking why somebody wants something will go a long way toward making the setting safe for the parties to speak as clearly and directly as they wish to.

Since the whole natural adversary relationship is primarily one of conflict, it should be relatively simple to get both parties to see and agree that conflict itself is okay. The trick is to set the guidelines so that conflict, when it occurs, will become more productive. For example, one way to keep conflict more controllable would be to adopt the rules for creative fighting in Chapter 9 as a part of the contract.

Once the contract is accepted, if anyone violates it, someone simply calls the offender on the violation and then asks that he reword his statement.

How demands will be made and answered. The one thing that adversaries have absolutely no experience with is supporting each other. If anything, their relationship is characterized by attempts to block and resist each other. With the change in conditions that has suggested that they need to find a way to work (or live) together also comes the change that they must begin to interact. Obviously, there is little point in going through this process if the result does not include some willingness to accede to each other's demands.

When the time comes for the adversaries to state their demands, using a somewhat formalized approach will help to keep the energy focused on the actions of the adversaries rather than on the adversaries themselves. They will probably have very strong tendencies to resist each other, since this is what both parties have the most skills in at the moment. Some points in the contract that will help to keep the situation workable are:

1. All demands must be introduced with the phrase "What I would like is. . . ."
2. All demands must be made to specific individuals.
3. All requests for clarity must be phrased in terms of "What" or "How," *never* "Why."
4. All responses to demands must be made using one of these three expressions: "Yes, I will," "No, I won't," "Yes, I will under the following circumstances. . . ."

Rules for disengagement. Meetings should be planned with strict, mutually agreed upon time limits. Once set, these time limits should be adhered to.

Futhermore, since both parties will probably be anticipating trouble, it is wise to build an escape clause into the contract so that if necessary, there is a means for separating temporarily without endangering the entire process. A typical contract point would state "Either party may disengage at any time. The disengaging person must, however, state his or her reason before leaving." Sometimes, tempers will flare, people will be preoccupied with other events, or there is just a little craziness in the air, and it is best to separate. Neither adversary should ever be forced to engage or to stay in the environment if he does not want to continue at that time.

For the times when normal disengagement occurs at the scheduled end of a meeting, one option is to have a contract point that says, "Each individual will end by giving a brief statement on how he or she sees things right now." This forces all parties to hear positive and negative points that both allies and adversaries have seen, and it keeps everyone up on how the process is going.

For example, when I was in high school, I belonged to a fraternity. The last business of every meeting was called "Good & Welfare." This was the only part of the meeting that was absolutely solemn. The chapter president would declare, "Good & Welfare," and the sergeant-at-arms would bar the door. The president would then start with the person in the first chair in the first row and ask, "Is there any Good & Welfare for Charlie?" Anybody could say anything that he wanted Charlie to hear. The recipient was allowed to say *nothing*! When that was complete, the president would move to the person in the next chair and ask, "Is there any Good & Welfare for Pete?" and so on.

As you can imagine, high school kids can get pretty close to the bone, and the feedback would be pretty brutal at times: Things said that would guarantee a sock in the jaw under any other circumstances were heard clearly and nondefensively in this unique situation. The result was clearer contact and functional relationships all the time.

Making Conflict Productive

Since the adversary relationship has grown out of the parties' resistance to making contact with each other, all the elements discussed in Chapter 6 are applicable here. The facilitator's prime objective is to get the adversaries to own, and take responsibility for, their resistance. The facilitator can best accomplish this by respecting the resistance as it surfaces. It is likely that most of the resistance that has contributed to the current adversary relationship is pseudo resistance, not authentic resistance. Each party's resistance to contact *now* must be surfaced safely and must be honored if it is eventually going to be lessened.

The number of these meetings generally depends on how intense the adversary relationship is. Once these initial meetings are completed, the facilitator has to determine whether both parties are authentically willing and ready to engage each other. Although this is a most important decision, it's not that difficult a judgment call. People eventually get tired of sitting on the bench and want to get in there and play. Once healthy engagement does occur, the facilitator's primary function is to "guard" the contract between the adversaries and to look for opportunities to move the action into the arena of productive conflict.

CHAPTER 12

Developing Power in Others *or* Lessons Learned from a Dead Lizard

Part of my ritual whenever I go to Miami to visit my folks is to spend every minute of the daylight hours stretched out in the sand, no more than 25 feet from the water. One afternoon during a visit several years ago, in my fourth hour of baking in the sun, I happened to open my eyes and notice a small lizard tenuously balancing himself on my sandal. He was about two and a half inches long, had lost his tail, had a scar down his back, and, if such a thing is possible, had a black eye. Clearly he was the most pathetic lizard ever to grace the face of the earth.

Since I am a member of the support professions, all my natural instincts to help came to the forefront. I had little doubt that if left in the hot sun, the little lizard would die. Thus I decided to transport him over the hot sand to a cool palm grove near the snack bar.

I picked up my sandal very gently in order not to dislodge him and began the long, very painful trek back to the grove. Since he was on my sandal, I had to accomplish this barefoot through sand hot enough to qualify me for instant adulthood in any primitive tribe in the world. But the pain I had chosen to endure made the act all the more noble. When I finally reached the grove, I very carefully set the sandal down in the shade of some tropical shrubbery. Feeling very good about myself, I stepped back to watch what would happen. The small lizard hung on to the thong for a few more moments and then very gingerly eased himself off the sandal and onto the ground—whereupon, a large lizard came out of the shrubbery and ate him!

I remember going through many different feelings quite rapidly. The first was the pure horror of it. Next came anger at the large lizard for murdering my client and then anger at the small lizard for allowing himself to be eaten, particularly after all that I had done for him. Then came sadness, some for the untimely demise of the lizard and some for the negative outcome of what was a really nice piece of work on my part. Finally came the philosophical adjustment of "What the hell, that's the way nature works."

It wasn't until sometime later that the real message of what had happened dawned on me. Not only wasn't I the poor, unthanked hero of the piece, I was the villain! First of all, at no time had the lizard ever asked me for help. In fact, it occurred to me that the small lizard probably spent a much longer, more difficult time getting to a place of relative safety in the hot sand than it took for me to take him back to the cool—but dangerous—palm grove. My biggest error, however, was my assumption that I knew what was best for the lizard.

It has been many years since that incident occurred. I have continued with my own development and have been quite active in working with managers and others in the support professions. However, no other incident has ever driven the point home more clearly to me on just what help and support *aren't*.

A central theme of this book is that you cannot empower or disempower anyone else, and nobody else can do this for you or to you either. All you can ever do is to empower, or disempower, yourself. What is available to you is the opportunity to support others in the process of self-empowerment. The primary objective of parenting is to assist your kids in developing their own strengths, competencies, and awareness of their self-worth. Along the way you diaper, feed, support, hold, buy for, teach, send notes for, car pool, and so on—all in service to the day when they walk out the door with a brief "Thanks, I can take it from here." As it is with parenting, so it is with managing. The roles are not really that much different. As a manager, your major function is to help strengthen your subordinates, because this is where the payoffs are for you. Stronger subordinates produce better results and are a justifiable source of pride.

Guidelines

This chapter presents several guidelines that can assist you in better supporting those whose strength is important to you.

Avoid Taking Responsibility for Others

Fritz Perls, the founder of Gestalt therapy, defined *maturity* as the reliance on internal, rather than external, resources. This definition does not imply that others' opinions are to be disregarded. On the contrary, it suggests that it is beneficial to be aware of whatever is affecting the situation at the time. The essence of the definition is that when all the relevant information is in, mature individuals will determine what is best for themselves. I can think of no better way of stating what the support role of the superior is to the subordinates in terms of empowerment than to say that the superior is there to help the subordinates to rely on their own, rather than on external, resources.

When a manager takes responsibility for another individual's welfare, several things occur that tend to hamper, rather than facilitate, a positive outcome. By taking responsibility for the welfare of another, you give the message that the other person is incapable and you deny that person the opportunity to take responsibility for his own welfare. Thus, after each supposedly supportive encounter with you, he is, paradoxically, less able to be self-supportive than before.

The ineffective manager or parent is like a crutch. He supports endlessly and compassionately, and as long as this goes on, the subordinate or child never needs to be self-supporting. The effective manager or parent is like a barbell; he uses skills, talent, and caring to help the subordinate or child increase his own sense of strength and self-worth.

The fact is that you have no ultimate responsibility for any adult other than yourself. To assume otherwise is sheer egotism. The best way to approach fulfilling your role of supporter of self-empowerment is from a base of reality. That is, by taking ultimate responsibility for yourself, you will be better able to facilitate others in doing the same for themselves.

The etymology of the word *responsibility* means "the ability to respond." There are some times when people do not have all the ability needed to deal with the problems or crises that they are facing. In these cases, your role is to facilitate a weaning process from dependence to independence, which is a learning experience. There may be times or situations where it is necessary for you to *temporarily* shoulder some of your subordinate's or child's responsibilities, because that individual is having a problem coping at the moment. In such cases there are several conditions that must be maintained for your external support to be effective. First, be sure that it is a temporary situation, with clear time boundaries if possible. Second, be sure that the support pertains to specific acts or functions. Third, be sure that the individual is willing to take as much responsibility for his own welfare as he is capable of handling under the circumstances. Even at this time of crisis, do not take full responsibility. Remember, you are *weaning* the individual, not taking over for him.

Avoid Giving Advice

I am unquestionably the world's foremost authority on me. Only I have unending consciousness of myself. Only I know the extent to which I value some things and discount others. Nobody is more concerned with my welfare or more frustrated by my screw-ups than I am. Under these conditions, it makes little or no sense for me to give my decision-making power and control to someone who does not possess this wealth of information.

Assuming that you know what is best for somebody else and then confidently giving the person your sound advice is a sure way of decreasing your impact on the other person. Advice giving is usually counterproductive for the following reasons. First, you clearly do not have as much information about the individual's welfare as she has. When she follows your advice, regardless of how sound it may appear, she has cut herself off from her own internal resource. Second, even when your intentions are the best, you have little to gain and a lot to lose if your advice is followed. If the advice is sound, the other person gets the credit; if the advice isn't sound, *you* catch the blame. Aside from the blame and the loss of credibility, you have no stake in the outcome whether your advice is followed or not. In the story I related at the beginning of this chapter, I ended up with a little psychic pain— the lizard ended up dead! The best assumption to make is that the other person is *safest* when she makes her own decisions. Third, there is no way to guard against projections when you are giving advice. As discussed earlier, projections are feelings of my own that I attribute to someone else. When you give advice, the implicaton is that you think you know what's best for the other person. The statement that starts out with "What you should do is . . . " almost always means "If I were you in this situation, what would be best for me is . . . , *so you go ahead and do what would best for me.*" Usually the advice giver isn't aware that this is what she is saying.

There is an alternative to advice giving that is effective and that supports the self-empowerment of the other person. This is to state your *opinion* clearly and succinctly and without ever implying that the other should see the situation the way you see it. There is no question that the other person and the situation become part of your world as you are working with her. To be in touch with that and to respond openly about how you see things is very productive. When you do this, what you bring to the other person is, first, your expertise with similar problems and, second, a totally different view or perspective that might represent a very viable alternative. It's really okay to share your hunches with the person about what's going on as long as you are both clear that what is being shared is your hunch and not an official pronouncement about how things really are. It is the other person's right and responsibility to accept or reject all or part of what you are suggesting. And when she is clear about this and, through making her own decisions, learns more about what she wants and what is going on, it becomes easier for you to give her the support she needs to obtain her goal.

As for me, I have developed an excellent defense against the chronic advice givers in my life. When anyone says to me, "Hank, if I were you, I'd . . . ," I immediately interrupt them with "If you were me, you would be doing *exactly* what I am doing right now."

Focus on What's Going Well

Managing and parenting are, more often than not, a problem-centered operation. People often come to you because they are in a state of distress or confusion and want or need help. In this environment it is very easy to concentrate only on the one negative aspect in the individual's situation that is causing problems. What is frequently lost to both the manager and the subordinate or the parent and the child is that in most cases many aspects of the individual's situation are going very well.

A trap to be avoided by the person supporting self-empowerment in others is the deification of change. Most supportive interventions are based on the unquestioned premise that change is good. I think that frequently change really is good and that how good it is depends on how the decision to change is made.

Instead of first looking for what needs to be changed in the person's situation, you and the individual should focus initially on how things are right now. If you help him to contact both extremes—that is, what is really going well and what is really not going well—he will be more in touch with the total picture and have more options available. From this stance it will be easier to identify those elements in his situation that would benefit from change and those that are serving very well right now and would be best left alone.

Do Nothing for Anyone That He Is Capable of Doing Himself

Many times an individual plays weak, stupid, or defenseless. By *playing,* I do not mean that this is an intentional or conscious attempt at manipulation (although sometimes it may be). Usually the individual is not aware that she is capable of accomplishing the task.

A subordinate, child, or trainee has every justification for going to you for help and/or guidance. Let's say you have a subordinate named Kate. A problem may arise when you simply give Kate the help and then encourage her to come back any time that there is a problem. Although your intentions in giving the help are good, the effects are quite damaging. First, although the immediate problem is solved, Kate is unaware of the process by which it was solved and is no more capable of solving a similar problem the next time it occurs. Second, you have inadvertently established yourself as the "authority" and the "keeper of the process." You are now really on the way to becoming a *superior* in Kate's eyes. The longer this goes on, the more established this relationship becomes, to the mutual detriment of both of you.

Your function is to assist Kate in becoming more capable of handling unique and difficult situations. One way to do this is to almost never answer a request for help directly. That is, when you are asked, "What should I do?" the best response is for you to ask, "What makes the most sense to you?" Even if Kate's initial response is totally incorrect, it's an opportunity to begin the training process, that is, to get Kate started on the path to self-reliance.

By way of example, when my son was much younger, he would occasionally come to me with a question about whether something was right or wrong. Instead of telling him, since I wasn't always so sure myself, I usually insisted that he give me his opinion first and then tell me why he thought the way he did. I would then give him my opinion, and we would discuss the similarities and differences. Although I didn't always agree with his position, the outcome is that he and I have always been able to communicate and that he has developed both a sound basic value system and self-reliance.

What it all boils down to is this simple imperative: If you *really* want to help, don't! Get the individual to help herself. Put the ball in her court by getting her to answer her own questions, at least at first.

Be Clear Yourself

One of my favorite movies is the classic, *Marty.* The picture deals with the life of a middle-aged bachelor in Brooklyn. One of the more memorable aspects is that Marty spends a fair amount of his life sitting around discussing with his buddies, "What do you want to do?" which is always answered with "I don't know. What do you want to do?" And that is pretty much all they do for the first half of the film.

One of the axioms of power is that strength breeds strength. That is, the clearer that I am about something, the clearer you will be. Marty is a character in a movie, but I can tell you that I have spent more time than I'd care to admit doing pretty much the same thing as Marty.

One of the best ways to assist people in getting clearer and stronger is to not collude with their confusion. If I am confused or unclear about what I want, that certainly will not help you in getting clearer about what you want. For instance, instead of my asking, "What would you like to do?" suppose I said, "I'd like to go to a movie, would you care to join me?" In this case you have something clear to respond to, and you will become clearer yourself. Thus you would either respond with "Yes," "No," or "How about . . . instead?" Regardless of the particular response, the result will be that both of us will be clearer and better off for the interchange.

Avoid Protecting People from Yourself

One of the myths that I held about myself in my late teens and early twenties (and I blush when I admit it) was that if I got really mad—I mean really, really mad and uncorked—the whole east coast would go as a result of the ensuing devastation. I even had some people semiconvinced that this might really happen. Although I was being authentic in this belief, I was also being a little bit silly.

The reality is that I have on occasion gotten mad. I mean really, really mad and uncorked, and, of course, you have firsthand knowledge that the east coast is still there and doing fairly well. Nobody died from my explosions, nobody ended up in a mental institution, and frankly ten minutes later there was rarely anybody who was really very interested, nor should there have been.

Your anger, your caring, your interest, or anything else that you are experiencing or feeling in reaction to any specific statement is a full statement of you. As discussed earlier, a full, contactful expression of yourself is essential in regaining and expressing power. This expression also has a very positive effect on the other person in terms of his rediscovering his own power.

First, being clear about who you are carries as much impact as being clear about what you want. For example, if you express excitement about what I am doing right now, I can contact and experience my own excitement about it more fully. Or if you express your anger at what I have just done, I can more readily see the impact of my action and more quickly ascertain my own level of responsibility.

Second, when you express yourself fully, you provide a model for effective behavior. If you raise your voice when you get angry, you "grant permission" and illustrate to me that under the circumstances this is an appropriate way to express anger. It is the same when you laugh when you're amused or ask a question when you're confused.

Third, and probably most important, when you allow me to experience you fully, you are telling me that, in your opinion, I am strong enough to handle you. How can I not take that as a mark of respect?

When you *overstate* a feeling, for example, express rage when annoyance is appropriate or express grief when sadness is appropriate, your lack of precision results in confusion, temporary loss of boundary, and sometimes fear in the other person. When you *understate* or withhold a full expression, for example, express simple approval when enthusiasm is appropriate or express mild pleasure when joy is appropriate, you literally rob the other person of experiencing you and your support for his own process of self-empowerment.

Support the Stronger, Work with the Weaker

The trend in human relations training today is to support the weaker and work with the stronger. This human relations position has resulted in some fine work. However, let me set up a hypothetical situation, based on several real experiences, to illustrate the difference in effects between this approach and my approach, which is to *support the stronger and work with the weaker*. First, the human relations approach:

The setting is a staff meeting. The players are the plant manager, his five department heads, their immediate subordinates, and the consultant (me). Suppose that in the middle of the meeting a more junior member says something inappropriate that enrages the plant manager. He turns to the junior member and reads him the riot act in front of the entire group, leaving the subordinate a broken, thoroughly humiliated wreck. In the role of human relations consultant, I would immediately go to the subordinate to give him some aid and comfort and to make sure that he is okay. I would then turn my attention to the plant manager and first get him to see that he won't be able to get much of a contribution from the subordinate in his current state. The objective here is to get the superior to view the effects of his behavior. I would then begin to work with the plant manager in finding softer or less aggressive ways of expressing his displeasure.

According to my own approach, after the confrontation I would ignore the plant manager (he's okay), and turn my total attention to the subordinate. I would disengage him from the group and then point out that despite the plant manager's blast and his feelings of humiliation, he is *literally* alive. After getting him calmed and a bit more secure, I would ask him, "Is there anything that you'd like to say to the plant manager?" If he answered in the affirmative, I would ask him to say it to me privately. After he had *contactfully* expressed his feelings to me, I would say, "The manager is right here. Do you want to say it to him?" Suppose the subordinate says yes and then says to the plant manager, "Sir, I may have been out of line; however, I would like you not to yell at me that way when I make a mistake"—whereupon the plant manager swings around and lets the subordinate have both barrels, leaving him, once again, a quivering mass. I now go back to the subordinate, disengage him from the group, and point out very clearly, "Now you're alive *twice!*"

Although the hypothetical situation is intentionally drawn just a little larger than life, hopefully it illustrates a major point. Both approaches work, but the tendency of the first is to weaken the stronger individual, and the tendency of the second is to strengthen the weaker one.

Bringing things a little closer to home, if your older kid has a tendency to pick on your younger one, you have two basic choices with regard to power. You can either concentrate your efforts on finding ways to control the older boy's aggressiveness or assist the younger one in discovering ways to protect and stand up for himself better, letting him know that he can always come to you if things get too difficult. My approach is almost always to say to the "winner," "Good for you, you got what you wanted," and then to work with the "loser" in terms of how he stopped himself from getting what he wanted.

Focus on the Choice, Not on the Action

Many people who have wanted to become stronger, clearer, or more powerful have decided or been advised to get formal training in assertiveness. There is nothing wrong with this, since many people have lost their awareness of their skills in this area. The problem is that along with the skills comes the message: "Now that you have the skills, *use them!*" The focus is on the action, and the skills are to be put to use whether or not the person feels ready to use them. I'm sure that in many instances this works well, because the person is ready, but in just as many cases the results are less than spectacular because the person isn't ready; that is, the person needs a little more time to get comfortable with the approach or a little more self-confidence.

Power does not reside in assertiveness or aggressiveness, *power resides in conscious choice.* If you are going to actively foster self-empowerment in your subordinates or children, you have to help them to be very, very clear about the distinction! In the hypothetical situation between the subordinate and the plant manager, had the subordinate said to me, "Hank, it doesn't fit for me to confront him now" this would have been every bit as powerful as was his choice to confront the plant manager at that time.

I have said many times that you are the world's foremost authority on you. As it is with you, so it is with those whom you are trying to support. The more that you can assist them in owning their own ability to take care of themselves *their way,* the faster will be the process of their self-empowerment.

Everyone knows that most kids eventually have to learn how to deal with a bully. If you tell your kid to stand up to the bully as soon as possible—that is, if you focus on the action—you run several risks. The first major risk is that if your kid does as you want, he could get his block knocked off. Second, the chance of this happening is greater because your son is responding to your sense of what will work, which obviously doesn't match his own. (If it did, he would already have stood up to the bully.) Third, if he chooses not to heed your advice, his burden is now doubled. Not only does he have to live with his fear of the bully and probably a loss of self-esteem, but also he now has to struggle with being seen as a coward in your eyes, which is even more painful. Although your intent in focusing on the action was to support your son and foster empowerment, the result is disempowerment and loss of self-esteem.

A more effective approach is to help your kid to honor both his topdog (anger) and his underdog (fear). The strategy is to help him to see the costs of confronting the bully right now and the costs of not confronting the bully now. The next step is to assist him, nonjudgmentally, in making a conscious choice as to what is in his best interests for right now. The final step is to support that decision no matter which one it is. If you continually use this approach of focusing on the choice, you heighten the chances that your child will eventually choose exactly the right action to permanently resolve the problem to his satisfaction.

Provide Empathy, Not Sympathy

Empathy refers to understanding what somebody else feels; it is a cognitive response. *Sympathy* refers to having a feeling in response to what somebody else feels; it is an emotional response.

Empathy is very contactful and is essential in working effectively with resistance, conflict, and adversary relationships. It is also essential in supporting self-empowerment in others. Some examples of empathic statements are: "I understand how you could feel that way," "You really seem pleased," "I'm aware that you are angry with me." Empathy is basically nonjudgmental and, as mentioned, it conveys an understanding of the other person's emotional state.

Sympathy implies a feeling, rather than an understanding, on the part of the listener. Sympathy can be a very appropriate response when the other person is in some kind of physical or emotional pain and when the response is authentic. Sympathy has a "narcotic" effect in that it temporarily lessens the pain and provides external support for the person who is currently having difficulty supporting herself. Like other narcotics, sympathy can be addictive. The more you get, the more you want, and the worse off you are for getting it.

Whereas empathy is basically nonjudgmental, sympathy usually implies support for the feeling and hints at an alliance. There is a "Poor baby, I'll take care of you" quality to most statements of sympathy. (Remember that that's okay when the other person really does need to be taken care of.) The worst form of sympathy is statements that give the message "I feel your pain." First of all, nobody can feel anybody else's pain, and second, these statements breed confluence and loss of boundary between the sympathizer and the person who is hurting. This is hardly supportive of another's self-empowerment.

In a case where your subordinate just got her pet project shot down, or your daughter got cut from the team, an empathic response is quite effective and appropriate. Saying something like "I know what that's like, I've been through it myself" honors the other person's pain and lets her know that you're there if you're needed. On the other hand, a sympathetic response such as "How awful for you. They had no right to do that to you" tends to increase her awareness of her pain and of having been injured. More damaging still, the sympathetic response encourages her to blame others for her mishap and to see herself as a victim. This precludes her from examining the possibility that the project might not have been as well thought out as it could have been or that she just didn't have what was needed to make the team this time, but with a little more training and hard work she could make it next year.

In its most destructive form, sympathy is actually used to brutalize, rather than to help, the other person. If the sympathetic response is not sincere, or if it is expressed too often or for too long a time, the other person may eventually hear the *real* message, which is: "You poor slob! Look at how much better off I am than you are!" This has roughly the same effect on interpersonal relationships as saying, "Ha, ha, I told you so!"

In our home, somebody who has had a bad day and who says so can pretty much expect to get a sympathetic ear and some good support. If I forget myself and mention it a second time, I incur the risk of someone yelling, "Pity party!" and then having to endure a chorus of "Poooor Daaddyy."

Encourage Selfness, Aggression, and Arrogance

My bet is that as you read the above heading, you were questioning either my sanity or my morality, or both. My experience has been that most parents and managers will go to considerable lengths to discourage their children and subordinates from valuing or expressing any or all of these conditions. They are generally discounted by society as being bad ways to be. However, if you discount them, you are discouraging self-empowerment. Let me deal with these, one at a time. Let's begin with a few definitions:

Selfness: I get what I want and exploit nobody.
Selfishness: I get what I want by exploiting others.
Selflessness: I get by, by exploiting myself.

Selfness. The term simply means that I will go after what I want and make every effort to hurt no one in the process. This is the prime statement of power.

Selfishness. The term means that if pain is unavoidable, and if it is my choice to decide which one of us will get hurt, it is with regret that I choose you. I don't think that this is a statement of immorality. I think that it addresses the real world. Frankly, if the positions were reversed, I would expect you to choose me, and I wouldn't think the worse of you for it. By way of example, if you and I were in contention for a promotion and you had the say as to who would get it, all things being equal, whom would you choose?

Being selfish is part and parcel of competition, which is an appropriate strategy of conflict under the right circumstances, such as in any professional sport. For example, can you imagine the winners of the Super Bowl being upset because the losers lost?

Selflessness is most valued by society and most responsible for self-disempowerment. If I put the immediate welfare of my son above my own welfare, this is not selflessness. I get more personal satisfaction out of his getting something than I would if I had gotten that thing for myself. Selflessness makes a virtue of always putting everyone's needs above your own. If you are going to foster and reinforce self-empowerment in others, you aren't going to be very successful if, at the same time, you encourage them to subordinate their needs to everyone else's.

Aggression.   Assertiveness training is seen as being positive (by me too), but training people to be aggressive would be looked upon with pure horror by most people. And that's really too bad!

Aggression is the active pursuit of what you want from the environment. Note the similarity between the definitions of power and of aggression. Aggression refers to the pursuit of what you want, and power refers to your ability to get it. There is a strong link between these two concepts. A vital part of supporting power in others is to help them to fully accept the truth that if they are going to increase their ability to get what they want from the environment, they are in most cases going to have to actively pursue their objectives.

Obviously, there are times when assertiveness will be an equally appropriate tactic, that is, stating clearly what you want and holding it there. In my experience, however, when push comes to shove, the aggressive person usually wins out over the assertive person. A powerful person needs to be skilled in both assertiveness and aggression.

Arrogance.   Arrogance is almost universally seen in a bad light. The simplest way for me to make the point that it is a trait to be encouraged is to define it and let you consider it in light of the definition. I define *arrogance* as supreme confidence in one's self-worth. Put in a more day-to-day context, you're only as good as you think you are. Please note that I am not making a virtue out of arrogance, or of the other concepts either, for that matter. What I am attempting to do is to bring them back into their rightful positions as appropriate ways to be. By way of contrast, being "humble" is also quite appropriate under certain circumstances. For example, if you were to ask me to expound on my ability as a musician, dancer, or mathematician, you would get a dose of humility that would probably embarrass a saint.

Selfness, aggression, and arrogance as defined here are essential elements of the act and support of self-empowerment. The trick to fostering power in another person is to legitimize these characteristics and then to coach the person in ways to express them contactfully rather than invasively. For instance, in encouraging selfness, the message is: Take care of your own needs first, but also stay aware of the needs of others. For aggression, the message is: If you want something, it's up to you to go after it and to do what it takes to get it. For arrogance, the message is: You have to believe in yourself if you want others to believe in you.

Take Care of Yourself First

If you are going to use yourself to support the process of self-empowerment in others, the first law is: Take care of yourself first! Even though this sounds terribly self-serving, this is an essential consideration if you are going to remain effective in this role. By focusing on your welfare first as you support another's growth, you are, first, being a role model for powerful behavior. If you don't buy the premise, why should your subordinate? Most important, however, is that by taking care of yourself first you are, paradoxically, being of greatest support to your subordinate. If I happen to be your prime source of support at this moment, by taking care of myself first, I am guarding *your* prime resource.

A good illustration of this is that on commercial airlines the flight attendants are very explicit in instructing travelers with small infants in how to use the oxygen system. They point out that in case of an emergency, the passenger is to put his or her oxygen mask on *first,* and then to attend to the needs of the child.

Another illustration comes from my own work in personal growth workshops and in consulting. When the client lays out the problem or situation, I choose the element in the situation that is of most interest to *me* to begin the work. In this way I keep my energy and awareness alive, and as long as that element is of interest to the client, the consultation will work.

But if I am confused, or maybe even a little bored, by what you are saying as we work together on your idea and I don't respond to my own discomfort for fear of upsetting you, I am damn poor support for you. How can I possibly help you to get clearer about your problem if I keep myself bored and confused?

A very important consideration in guarding your own effective-ness as you support the power in another is to work from the zone of creative indifference. Since this term is pure, unadulterated psycho-babble, and there is no other term for it, let me explain. The *zone of creative indifference* can be thought of as the space that separates you from the other person as you are working with, or supporting, him or her. This is obviously psychological space, but it operates no differ-ently from physical space. For example, you couldn't get much work done if you were sitting in the subordinate's lap, nor could you accomplish much if you were attempting to communicate from 30 feet away.

Think of the zone as a river with a bridge crossing it. The subordinate is standing on one shore. If you are going to be maximally effective, you have to stay on the bridge. If you cross to the subordi-nate's shore, you are going to be too close and of very little assistance. You can generally tell when you have crossed over to the subordinate's side by such clues as finding yourself caring more about his progress than he does, becoming impatient with him or with the process because it isn't going fast enough to suit you, or becoming aware that you are more active in the process than he is. One signal that I became aware of that I was crossing the zone was when I found myself sitting forward in my chair, leaning into my client. When you cross the zone in this way, you have become confluent with the subordinate and are beginning to take responsibility for his welfare.

When you cross the zone in the other direction and get off on the opposite shore, you are too distant from the other person to be of any value. In this case, you really don't care very much and are there as a mechanical, rather than as a personal, resource. The other person could get just as much help from reading a book, in that you are in no position to make any personal impact.

Your ability to be good support for someone in any context, including the process of self-empowerment, depends most on your ability to make and maintain good contact.

CHAPTER 13

A Closing Note
on Risk and Power

Risk and its relationship to power and the increased effectiveness of the individual have been mentioned throughout this book. It is impossible to express power without incurring risk in the process. And since all power resides in the conscious choice among at least three alternatives, the first risk is always that you will reject a better alternative.

Risk

You can think of risk in terms of what you stand to lose if your attempt at power fails. The loss is estimated in relation to the status quo, that is: If I go ahead with the plan, what can I lose that I now have? The failure of the plan itself is not a part of estimating the risk because a failed attempt has the same result as no attempt. In determining risk, you need to consider three elements. First, what are the costs or risks for making no change? Second, what do you risk losing that you now have if failure occurs? Third, what are the chances for success or failure? Also, keep in mind that if you are completely successful in the attempt, you will have some new risks or costs that come with the new situation.

Suppose that Charlie is the subordinate manager and that Pete is the superior and that Charlie feels that Pete is undervaluing his contribution and not giving him the recognition that he deserves. What Charlie clearly wants is for Pete to give him this recognition. The question for Charlie becomes, "Should I confront Pete, and tell him how I feel about this situation?"

The first thing for Charlie to consider is what the risks are for no change. Some potential risks here for not confronting Pete are Charlie's continuing to feel undervalued, more distancing between Pete and Charlie, and a growing resentment on Charlie's part. The second thing for Charlie to consider is what he would lose, or risk losing, that he now has if he confronts Pete. Some possible losses are Pete's respect, finding out that Pete doesn't really care, and even Pete's questioning of Charlie's strength and stability.

The third thing for Charlie to consider is the chances of success or failure. Charlie has to estimate the probabilities in terms of what is happening at the moment, for instance, the quality of Pete and Charlie's personal relationship or whether Pete is under any external pressures that could be distracting him. If Charlie decides to proceed with the plan in view of the risks and the plan is successful, he must remember that there are new risks that come with going ahead with the plan. For example, Pete will be more aware of Charlie, which could lead to closer supervision, more work, or other changes that Charlie might not have wanted. There is really no way to avoid risk; you risk failing when you take the chance, and you risk missing an opportunity when you do not. We all face risk every day of our lives. Every time we say yes to something or someone, we say no to something or someone else. And every time we say no to something or someone else, we again take the risk of losing out on what a yes might have gotten us. Unfortunately, many people are not aware of the risk side of daily living.

There are three categories of risk takers. The first category includes those people who appear to make quick choices with highly successful results. Note that I said *appear* to make quick choices. Their high success rate is a clue to us that these people are aware of and understand the risks involved and that they weigh them before they make their decisions. It has been through practice, throughout their lives, and through surviving some failure that they are now able to rapidly go through the process of becoming aware, understanding, and choosing. But even these people take more time when they are faced with decisions that carry more and heavier risks.

The second category of risk takers is made up of people who seem to be completely unaware, either from a lack of understanding or knowledge or from an inability to learn from experience, that there are always risks involved in any choice. These people seem to have a very low success rate, and when they are successful, they usually experience this condition only temporarily. Typically these are the individuals who are working on their fourth major in college or their fifth business venture or their sixth marriage. Their few successes are due mainly to chance. In effect, these individuals have an underdeveloped underdog; they simply do not seem to be aware that the risks are there.

The third category of risk takers includes those people who are aware of the risks involved in every decision but who freeze themselves into immobility out of fear that no matter what they do, what is at risk is sure to be the result. Each time that these people avoid making a clear choice because of the risks involved, their feelings of vulnerability and of loss of control increase. These individuals have an overdeveloped underdog; the only thing that they seem to respond to in any choice situation is the element of risk.

Although we can easily talk of three discrete categories of people and some people will fit neatly into one of the three, the reality is that most of us probably spend some time in each one of them. How much time we spend and over which specific issues depend on what is occurring and what our particular styles are.

Many people have failed unnecessarily in a risk-taking situation because they did not properly figure out what the costs were ahead of time (as in telling the boss where to get off in a staff meeting), or because they did not calculate the probability of failure (as in betting one's life savings on the turn of a card), or because they were simply not in touch with what was going on in the environment or with whom they would be dealing (as in the air traffic controllers' strike of 1981).

A Debriefing Exercise

I'd like to introduce you to a debriefing exercise similar to the one that I use in most of my training workshops. Using it will increase your understanding of, and your ability to maintain control over, the risk factors involved in making choices and decisions. The exercise is done in two phases.

Phase 1.   First, get a pad and a pencil. Think back over the issues and the examples that were discussed in this book. Write out as many *complete sentences* as you can that begin with the words "I learned . . ." or "I learned that (I). . . ."

In this exercise, going for quantity will get you quality. These statements can come from anywhere. They can be related to something that I said in the text, or they can have nothing to do with anything that I said. If two statements are 90 percent similar, that's okay, because you are saying something that is 10 percent different, and differences are always what we're looking for. *Do not refer back to the book.* Rely on your memory to pull out what was important for you. Write as many complete statements as you can in ten minutes or until you run out of statements, whichever occurs first. What you are doing here is taking the "skim" off the top. When you have finished this list, go to Phase 2.

Phase 2. Phase 2 is a five-step process. Each step requires a "go/no go" decision at its completion before going on to the next step. If at any point your decision is "no go," go back and start again with Step 1.

Step 1. *"What do I want to do?"* Referring strictly to your list of "I learned . . ." statements from Phase 1, determine one thing that you are going to *do* to get something that you want that you do not now have. This can be from the work setting, the home, or any place else. Start with three things that sound good; then choose the best of the three.

Step 2. *"Who else will be affected by this?"* Write down the names of the individuals who will be affected in some way if you go ahead with this decision. Don't put down "Nobody." As a manager or a family member, it is impossible for you to do anything that will not have some impact on other people. If it's a "no go," for example, if you realize it could give a colleague some problems, go back to Step 1 and pick another objective to pursue. If it's a "go," and you see it won't affect your colleagues negatively, those colleagues may serve as a support group for enacting the plan set out in Step 1.

Step 3. *"What costs or risks accrue to me for doing this?"* Get in touch with what the potential costs or risks are to you if you go ahead with this. Write the risks down. Don't put down "None." If there were no costs or risks associated with doing this, you would probably have done it already.

Step 4. *"What costs or risks accrue to me for* not *doing this?"* Get in touch with what opportunities will be lost if you do not go ahead with this. Write them down. Don't put down "None." If there weren't any costs or risks for not attempting this, you wouldn't just be thinking about doing it, you'd be doing it. You are now at the point of conscious choice. That is, you know what it will cost you to do this and what it will cost you not to do it. *Choose!*

Step 5. *"When am I going to do it?"* If you decided to go ahead with the plan, write down the day and time that you intend to initiate it. Don't put down "First chance I get" or "Sometime next month" or "As soon as the smoke clears." Commit to a specific day and time. If something comes up that makes that day unfeasible, cross it out and put in a new day and time. Keep yourself honest.

In working on Step 1, determining the action you are going to take, I suggest that you keep the following four criteria in mind.

Select an action or objective that:

1. Will benefit you personally.
2. Is a relatively easy thing to do or accomplish.
3. Has a very high probability for success.
4. Has a minimal amount of risk or cost associated wtih it. That is, if you don't succeed at it, the worst thing that will happen to you is that you might look a little foolish or somebody might be momentarily upset with you.

If you complete this exercise as suggested and you are successful, the chances are that you will try it again. After all, as every poker player knows, the first law of poker is "Never quit a winner."

If you are successful again, do it again! Focus on what you want *now*, and start with Phase 2. If you continue to use this process over time, there are two things that you are likely to discover. First, you will find that you have markedly increased your power in terms of getting more of what you want from the environment. Second, on the eighth or ninth run of this, the minimal risk that you will be contemplating taking will be a risk that probably would have frightened you into immobility had you considered it on the initial run.

What I am referring to here, and what this exercise is about, is the process by which intelligent, grounded risk-taking behaviors are developed. The pure topdog takes every risk regardless of the potential costs. The pure underdog doesn't take any risks regardless of the potential gains. The integrated, powerful approach to risk taking is to first be very clear about what it is that you want. Next, assess the risk that you are willing to take to get it under the current circumstances. Finally, take only that risk, and not one that is even a little bit greater.

And So, Finally . . .

There are two major risks that are incurred in reading this book. The first is that you will finish the book, put it down, and go on a self-improvement crusade, swearing a mighty oath—"I'll never be powerless again!" Please avoid doing this if at all possible. Chances are that if you do this, you'll seem abrupt or uncaring rather than powerful. Remember that power resides in conscious *choosing*, not in what the specific choice is. The dependent person always says yes. The counter-dependent person always says no. The powerful, independent person chooses the appropriate response in light of the available alternatives.

If you embark on a self-improvement crusade, you also, paradoxically, risk becoming *less* powerful. If you turn the views and alternatives discussed in this book into a new set of "shoulds," it won't serve you any better than your old set of "shoulds." Remember that power is the natural state. As with all other things natural, you can't make them happen, you have to let them happen. If you actively pursue power, as discussed here, it will probably elude you.

A line from the "Desiderata" has always stuck in my mind: "You are a child of the Universe, no less than the trees and the stars; you have a right to be here." Go easy with this material and with yourself. The next time you look back on an event where you blew it, instead of damning yourself for giving your power away, I'd like you to congratulate yourself—first, for allowing your underdog to take care of you, even though it turned out that you really didn't need protecting this time, and second, for being aware that a choice point had occurred. If you stay aware each time that you miss a choice point, the probability that you will miss the next choice point decreases. And if, or when, you do miss the next one, the time between the event and your awareness that you missed it definitely decreases. The result is that relatively soon the event and the awareness that a choice can be made here occur simultaneously and naturally. Let it happen!

The second risk incurred in reading this book is that you will see power as the only, or the most important, aspect of living a full life. Please don't do this either. As mentioned in the Preface, power is one facet of good living. Being powerful is no more important than any other facet that contributes to happiness or success, such as being fun-loving, caring, or ethical. Nor is being powerful any less important than any other facet.

Power

If I could make a wish, my wish for you and every reader of this book would be:

1. To view power for what it is, a means to getting more of what you want for yourself and for those who are important to you in the home and work settings. Power is not an end in itself, nor does it have anything to do with domination, greed, or diminishing other people.

2. To recognize that the path to power is the ability to make and maintain solid contact with people and conditions in the environment. Contact is based on two elements. The first is maintaining a constant and clear I-boundary, that is, being aware of and valuing who and how you are. The second is the ability to stay in the here-and-now.

3. To remember that all power resides in conscious choice. The specific choice itself is secondary to the act of choosing. It is always the situation that determines what is appropriate and what is effective.

4. To constantly stay aware that you have responsibility for exactly one person on this planet—yourself. And to recognize that meeting this responsibility is a full-time job. Since you are absolutely unique and perfect the way you are, you need never apologize for yourself or feel that you are less than anyone else simply because that person would prefer you to be someone different. That person's approval of you may be desirable, but it must be of secondary importance to your own approval of you.

5. To remember that although you are accountable for your actions, you are never accountable to anyone for what you feel or for what you want. You choose your own friends and make your own enemies, and you have no responsibility for other people's relationships or their personal choices. Nobody owns anybody! We come together by choice and we part the same way.

6. To see that disempowerment is something that you do to yourself and that there aren't any real victims. You do not have the ability to empower or disempower anyone else. More important, no one has the ability to empower or disempower you.

7. To remember that when disempowerment occurs, it is usually because you have a desire to please or be more like someone else. Be more like yourself; this will truly please the people who are worth pleasing.

8. To stay in touch with the fact that to get what you want, you first have to know what you want. Once you are clear on this, the power to get those things for yourself depends on your capacity and willingness to state things clearly and to be willing to pursue them actively. The strategy is not to wrest that which belongs to someone else but, rather, to claim what is clearly yours or that which is unclaimed that you wish to make yours.

9. To understand the nature of resistance and see it for what it is, another way of expressing power. Remember that your own resistance protects you and serves your organization and that other people view their resistance the same way, even when they are resisting you or what you want. Honoring and working with others' resistance get you more than attempting to break it down, avoid it, or minimize it.

10. To remember that rejection, although painful, is sometimes unavoidable and is never terminal. And just as you must on occasion suffer the pain of rejection, you must also on occasion be willing to reject for your own welfare and for the welfare of the other person.

11. To not fear and avoid conflict, but instead to see it as a natural condition among strong people with different views. Use conflict as a source of energy and creativity instead of attempting to avoid or suppress it, for the reality is that conflict is with you whether you honor it or not. Remember that with conflict, as with any other form of interaction you choose to engage in, you have the ability to conduct it and control it.

12. To see the ability to creatively fight as a necessary skill for positive interaction. Remember that the goal of creative fighting is to gain an objective without damaging the opponent or the organization and to do so through authentic fighting.

13. To have a better understanding of what adversary relationships are, and how they emerge. Remember that although there will always be adversary situations and conditions because we all see things differently, there need never be adversary relationships. Even though adversary relationships do exist and are even seen as being natural, there is nothing natural about them. They emerge mostly from ego pain and are reinforced through societal myths and organizational blunders. Most important, remember that you can do things to avoid them and you can deal with those that are in existence.

14. To understand that almost everyone prefers success to failure, fun to boredom, and challenge to drudgery. People, by nature, are not perverse. Those who appear perverse may not be aware that they have other options. If they were trained in inappropriate behavior, they can also be weaned away from it.

15. To be aware that strength breeds strength and power breeds power. To foster power in others, you must first be comfortable with your own power and then you must use your power to help others to rediscover their own power.

16. To remember that power is the natural state. We have learned how to get along well, how to subordinate our needs, and how to disempower ourselves. But no one has to learn how to be powerful, contactful, or effective. These abilities are your birthright.

Acknowledgments

Throughout this book I have acknowledged input whenever I could remember the source as I was writing, but intentionally made no formal citations. There are some, however, that I would like to formally acknowledge here.

First, a blanket acknowledgment to the faculty of the Gestalt Institute of Cleveland for the enormous amount of effort and caring that they showered on me during my training with them in the early seventies.

I specifically want to acknowledge the work of Ed Nevis of the Gestalt Institute of Cleveland in the area of resistance. Ed's work laid the foundation for my own in the chapters dealing with resistance in this book.

My thinking in developing the strategies and tactics to deal with resistance has been influenced by Ed, by my exposure to the supervisory training programs developed by Development Dimensions International in Pittsburgh, Pennsylvania and Communispond of New York City, and the early work on discipline by Norman Meier.

The emphasis on personal growth needs in the work setting is certainly a result, in part, of my exposure to Fred Herzberg during my graduate school years.

I particularly want to thank Ed Cross for his constant encouragement, and Rob Kaplan for knowing a good thing when he saw it and not letting it go. A special word of appreciation goes to Bob and Mary Lewis Ash for their help and forbearance.

Thanks to Linda Reiman for her thoughtful work in copyediting this book. I also appreciated the editorial suggestions made by Janet Frick, Eva L. Weiss, and Richard Gatjens. I'd like to acknowledge Lydia Lewis, who designed the book.

Most important, I want to acknowledge the many contributions of my wife, Jeri, who, along with our son, Eric, provided a good deal of the anecdotal material and whose greatest contribution came in reading the first drafts. Her constant demand of "What the hell does *this* mean?" forced me to rethink and clarify a lot of material that would have gotten lost otherwise.

Finally, to all those who have read this book and said, "I told him that!" you're probably right. Please accept my thanks, and my apology for not remembering.

Index

HANK KARP received his Ph.D. in Industrial and Organizational Psychology from Case Western Reserve University and has completed postdoctoral work in Gestalt Therapy at the Gestalt Institute of Cleveland. After 10 years on the management faculty of Old Dominion University, he formed his own consulting firm, Personal Growth Systems, in 1979. American Can Company, I.B.M., Marathon Paper Company, Chaparrel Steel, and Mobay Chemical are among his clients.

Dr. Karp has designed public seminars for managers in a wide variety of areas, from leadership skill development to motivation and job enrichment. He frequently conducts public workshops for people in the helping professions in addition to running his own personal growth groups. He has published articles in various professional magazines and journals.